St. Benedict's Bones

St. Benedict's Bones

A Medieval Monastic Mystery

Jacobus de Voragine
Adrevald of Fleury
Peter the Deacon

Edited and translated by
Robert Nixon

RESOURCE *Publications* • Eugene, Oregon

ST. BENEDICT'S BONES
A Medieval Monastic Mystery

Resource Publications
An Imprint of Wipf and Stock Publishers
199 W. 8th Ave., Suite 3
Eugene, OR 97401

www.wipfandstock.com

PAPERBACK ISBN: 978-1-6667-3742-4
HARDCOVER ISBN: 978-1-6667-9685-8
EBOOK ISBN: 978-1-6667-9686-5

MARCH 21, 2022 9:06 AM

Contents

Translator's Introduction

This lowly monk took al in pacience,

And seyde, "I wol doon al my diligence,

As fer as sowneth into honestee,

To tellé yow a tale, or two, or three."

—Chaucer

St. Benedict of Norcia (480–547) is indisputably one of the most influential figures in the development of the culture and spirituality of Western Europe. Recognized as the "patriarch of all monks of the West" and the patron saint of Europe, with great wisdom and charisma he promoted the coenobitic movement in the Occident at the beginning of the Middle Ages. This monastic movement spread and expanded rapidly, and came to play a central role in the organization of Western society for the next thousand years. In our own times, there has been a renewed interest in and appreciation of Benedict's ideas. Many contemporary readers have found Benedictine principles and approaches to be of value not only in nurturing contemplative spirituality, but also in developing responsive and flexible leadership approaches, fostering supportive and compassionate community dynamics, and cultivating a holistically balanced and well-integrated lifestyle.

But although many aspects of medieval piety continue to resonate with contemporary spiritual seekers, it must be admitted that some of them may seem distinctly strange or curious. One such element of medieval piety was the veneration of the relics of saints. Such relics could range from fragments of clothing, to small portions of bone or hair, to the entire bodies of holy men and women. The question of the genuine location of the mortal remains of popular saints was often seen as a very important issue, and heated and complex disputes about such questions arose from time to time. Foremost amongst these was certainly the controversy about the location(s) of the body of St. Benedict and his twin sister, St. Scholastica, which the learned Mabillon describes as a "*gravissima et famosissima quaestio*" ("a most grave and famous question.")[1]

According to the earliest and most reliable biography of Benedict, traditionally attributed to Pope Gregory the Great, the saint died at the monastery at Monte Cassino (about eighty miles southeast of Rome), and was buried there, together with Scholastica, who had predeceased him by a few weeks.[2] Less than four decades after Benedict's death (that is, in about 580 or 581), the monastery fell prey to Lombard invaders and its monastic community was expelled. This event was apparently predicted by St. Benedict himself, who foretold not only the plundering and suppression of the monastery at Monte Cassino, but also the fact that none of the monks there would be killed in this invasion. In the second book of the *Dialogues* of Gregory the Great one reads:

1. Mabillon and d'Archery, *Acta Sanctorum Ordinis S. Benedicti*, 323.

2. It is to be noted that the reliability of the attribution of the *Dialogues* to St. Gregory has been questioned by some scholars. Apart from issues of the manuscript tradition of the work and certain apparent anachronisms, the *Dialogues* (the second of which contains the life of St. Benedict) present an episodic series of striking and sometimes fantastical miracles in a style which (arguably) lacks the usual literary polish of Gregory's writing, and bears much closer affinity to the raconteurial style of Gregory of Tours. See Clark, *The Pseudo-Gregorian Dialogues,* and Vogüé, "Is Gregory the Great the Author of the *Dialogues*?"

> A certain nobleman called Theoprobus was converted to monastic life by the good counsel of St. Benedict. Because of his virtue and merit of life, he enjoyed a close familiarity with the holy man. One day, coming into Benedict's cell, he found the saint weeping very bitterly. After waiting expectantly for a good while and observing that Benedict did not cease from his weeping, Theoprobus asked him the cause for his great sorrow. Benedict answered in tones of deep melancholy, saying, "All of this great Abbey [of Monte Cassino] which I have built, and all the things which I have so diligently prepared for my brother monks here, shall be—by the judgement of almighty God—given over into the hands of the pagans, to be looted and overthrown! But by my prayers, God has promised me to spare the lives of those monks that should be living in this monastery at the time."
>
> The prophetic utterance which Theoprobus then heard, we ourselves have witnessed [in our own times] to have come true.[3] For we know that the monastery of Monte Cassino was indeed devastated and suppressed by the Lombards. One night, when the monks were all asleep, these barbarian raiders entered the monastery by force and looted all its possessions. However, not one single person amongst all the monks was captured or harmed by them; rather, thanks be to God, they all escaped from the attack safe and sound. Thus almighty God fulfilled what he promised to his faithful servant, Benedict: for though he permitted the Lombards to seize the monastic house and all the goods therein, he mercifully preserved the lives of the monks.[4]

Fortunately for the Benedictine monastic order, however, approximately a century and a half later the ruined and deserted monastery of Monte Cassino was restored and re-opened. This revival was brought about largely through the efforts of St. Petronax (670–747) who became the first abbot of the restored

3. Gregory (or pseudo-Gregory) was writing this in the late sixth century, shortly after the Lombard invasion.

4. Gregory, *Vita S. Benedicti*, 168.

establishment, supported by the encouragement and authority of Pope Gregory II (715–731).[5]

It is at about this point that the controversy of the location of Benedict and Scholastica's mortal remains arises. According to one tradition, after the monastery had been devastated by the Lombards and lay abandoned, the bodies of both Benedict and Scholastica were removed and relocated to France. According to another tradition, this relocation never occurred at all, but rather their bones were, in due course, rediscovered at Monte Cassino. The actual events themselves necessarily remain shrouded in the mystery of the elapsed centuries. But even to this day, both Fleury Abbey at Saint-Benoît-sur-Loire, France, and Monte Cassino Abbey, Italy, claim to possess the mortal remains of St. Benedict. Thankfully, these rival claims are now of an entirely friendly nature.

This volume presents, for the first time in English, two key medieval works relating to the mystery of the location of St. Benedict's body. The first is *The Tale of the Relocation of the Bodies of St. Benedict and St. Scholastica into France* (*Historia Translationis S. Benedicti et S. Scholasticae in Galliam*), written during the ninth century by Adrevald, a monk of Fleury in France.[6] The second work is *The History of the Discovery of the Bodies of St. Benedict and St. Scholastica at Monte Cassino* (*Historica Relatio de Corpore S. Benedicti Casini*), by Peter the Deacon, a monk and librarian to the monastery at Monte Cassino writing in the twelfth century.[7] These documents offer alternative, and indeed radically conflicting, versions of the events. The first relates how the remains of Benedict and Scholastica were discovered in Italy by a party of French monks, then taken back to France to be installed at Fleury and Le Mans respectively. The second, in explicit contradiction to the first, describes the remarkable discovery of the undisturbed tomb of Benedict and Scholastica in the church of Monte Cassino

5. See Mabillon, *Annales Ordinis S. Benedicti*, 56.

6. Avelard, *Historia Translationis*, 901–910.

7. The source of the Latin text for this document is the *Acta Sanctorum, Martii, Tomus Tertius*, 288–297.

in the latter part of the eleventh century, and the series of miraculous occurrences which follow.

The question of the historical veracity of these two narratives is almost certainly of less pressing concern to most modern readers (whether monks or non-monks) than it would have been to their medieval, monastic counterparts. Nevertheless, the surviving narratives of both stories are fascinating and richly rewarding documents, filled with many astonishing events and remarkable miracles. Within these pages, the reader will encounter fierce barbarian hordes, adventurous quests to discover ancient tombs, ferocious dragons, man-eating wolves, mysterious visions, and enigmatic oracles. Here will be found tales of saints fleeing from papal forces under the shroud of darkness, phantasmagoric apparitions of dead monks, malicious poisonings, nocturnal attacks made on infants by venomous toads, levitating lamps, and a veritable multitude of other marvels.

A translation of the account of the life of St. Benedict from the thirteenth-century *Legenda Aurea* (*Golden Legend*) of Jacobus de Voragine is also included, as a preface to the two historical narratives.[8] This version of the saint's life is clearly derived from that of Gregory the Great. It omits very little of the narrative content of the longer and much better-known work, but has a certain piquancy typical of the concise and vibrant popular style cultivated by Jacobus.

The translational approach adopted here is one of dynamic equivalence, conveying the sense of the original in (hopefully) acceptably idiomatic English. In the great many cases where the original Latin text is unclear, fragmented, disjointed, or otherwise infelicitous, a degree of literary liberty and paraphrastic polishing has been exercised to produce a more readily digestible rendition for the contemporary anglophone reader. The passages in verse are, of course, free adaptations. Footnotes have been added to provide details of historical or geographical context, or to comment on textual issues, wherever this seems helpful.

8. Jacobus, *Legenda Aurea*, 157–159.

In compiling and presenting these fascinating and curious works, the objective is certainly not to solve the ancient and long-running mystery of the true location of St. Benedict's body (which has become itself a venerable part of the Benedictine heritage), but rather to offer a pleasant and illuminating insight into a remarkable and colorful world of medieval legend, wonder, and intrigue. May this be an edenic garden of diversion and delight to the reader, even as it has been to me,

The humble translator,

Fr. Robert Nixon, OSB
Abbey of the Most Holy Trinity,
New Norcia, Western Australia

1

The Life of St. Benedict, from the *Golden Legend*

BY JACOBUS DE VORAGINE

(C.1230–1298)

St. Benedict's Bones

St. Benedict, whose name means "blessed," has this particular name either because he imparted blessings to many people and many things; or because he himself enjoyed many blessings during his life; or because all were blessed on account of him; or because he deserves to have eternal blessings in Heaven. His life was written by St. Gregory the Great.

❋ ❋ ❋

Benedict was born in the province of Norcia,[1] and from there was sent to Rome to pursue a liberal education, according to usual custom. But whilst still a child, he abandoned his literary studies and resolved to seek the solitude in order to lead a life of contemplation and prayer. He therefore went forth alone, accompanied only by his nurse (who loved him dearly), and arrived at a place called Affile.[2]

Having arrived there, his nurse obtained a sieve with which to winnow wheat. But she happened to place this sieve on a table somewhat carelessly, and it fell to the floor and broke cleanly into two parts. Benedict saw his nurse weeping over this accident, and was at once moved to pity towards her. Taking the fractured sieve, the holy boy prayed over it intently. And, lo, it was restored to perfect completeness in the twinkling of an eye, as if it had never been damaged!

A little later, Benedict secretly fled from his nurse and went off completely alone. He arrived at a certain place and remained

1. Norcia is approximately one hundred miles north-east of Rome. According to other sources, Benedict was born to the noble Anicius family, and was thus related to Boethius, St. Gregory the Great, Pope Felix III, and many other illustrious personages. His father was Eupropius and his mother was Abundantia.

2. According to other sources, Benedict was fourteen years of age when he left Rome to pursue the eremitic life. The name of his nurse was Cyrilla. Some sources indicate that Benedict's mother died whilst he was still an infant (or even in childbirth), and that Cyrilla had nursed and raised him (together with Scholastica) in place of his mother. According to Gregory's version of his life, whilst at Affile (a location about thirty miles east of Rome) he took up residence in a church dedicated to St. Peter.

there for three years.[3] During this period he had no human contact, with the single exception of a monk by the name of Romanus. This Romanus sedulously provided Benedict with all the necessities of life.

Now, Benedict dwelt in a deep cave which it was not possible for Romanus himself to reach. So it was his practice to attach a basket containing bread to a rope and to lower it to the hermit. He also attached a small bell to the rope, so that the man of God would hear its tinkling and know when supplies were being lowered to him. But the devil, the ancient enemy, was filled with envy at both the charity of Romanus and the refreshment and sustenance being received by Benedict. So the arch-fiend maliciously hurled a stone at the bell and shattered it to pieces! Nevertheless, the diligent Romanus refused to be deterred or frightened by this, and continued to supply the holy hermit with his needs.

Some time afterwards, the Lord appeared to a certain priest who was preparing a festive meal for himself to celebrate Easter. And God said to him, "Here you are, preparing a feast of fine delicacies for your own consumption, whilst my servant, Benedict, is tormented by hunger!" Upon hearing this, the priest was filled with compunction. He arose and went off to find the saint, taking the food with him. Eventually (and with some difficulty) he located him, and said, "Arise, my brother! Let us eat together, for this is the day of Easter."

To this Benedict replied, "Verily, I now know that it is Easter, for I have received the blessing of your visit!" Indeed, at that time the saint was leading an isolated life and had no other way in which he could have known that it was Easter on that day. The priest said to him, "Since it is now the feast of the Lord's Resurrection, it does not behoove us to be sparing with food or drink! Therefore I have come to you so that we may celebrate together." And, blessing God, the hermit and the priest enjoyed a fine Easter banquet that day.

3. According to St. Gregory's account, this place was beside a lake and was therefore known as "*Sub lacu*" (Subiaco). It is located about forty miles from Rome.

❁ ❁ ❁

One day as Benedict was out walking, a certain species of black bird, known as a "merle," began to fly around his face in a most annoying manner. And so persistently and closely did the bird plague him that he would have been able to capture it in his hand had he so wished. But instead, the saint made the sign of the cross, and at once the bird departed from him.

The devil then tempted him in another form, by drawing before the eyes of his mind the image of a certain very attractive woman whom he had previously seen. This ignited such a flame of desire in the heart of the hermit that he seriously considered departing from the solitude, and abandoning his life of prayer and contemplation altogether. But suddenly, thanks to the intervention of Divine Grace, he returned to his better senses and recalled his earnest vows and intentions. Then he threw himself into some nettle bushes which were close at hand, and rolled himself back and forth vigorously. The wounds which he suffered thereby on his body served to cure the wound of fleshly temptation which had afflicted his mind, and the smarting sting of the thorns upon his skin served to extinguish the burning flame of lust in his heart. And from that time, Benedict was never again tempted by carnal desires or concupiscence of the flesh.

❁ ❁ ❁

Benedict's renown for wisdom and sanctity became ever greater as time went by. Now it happened that the abbot of a certain nearby monastery passed away. And the entire community of monks there then went to Benedict, and implored him to lead them as their new abbot. For a long time he was very reluctant to agree to this proposal, saying that his own manner of life and theirs did not accord at all well. But at last he was overcome by their entreaties and supplications, and consented to become their abbot.

Having assumed this position, Benedict very soon perceived that they did not observe many of the rules of monastic life, and he duly reproved them for their shortcomings with paternal care. But as a result of this, many of the monks began to regret that they had asked Benedict to lead them, for they realized that their dissipated way of life would not be tolerated by the saint. When they saw what they had previously been accustomed to do freely was now no longer permitted to them, they resolved to rid themselves of their new abbot, by fair means or foul. So some of them secretly mixed some poison in with wine. This they brought to Benedict as he was seated at the table. But he made the sign of the cross over it, and at once the glass goblet which contained the wine shattered, as if it had been struck by a rock! He then realized that the wine had been poisoned—that it was indeed a cup of death, since it was not able to withstand or resist the cross, which is the sign of eternal life.

The saint then arose and, with a placid and serene face, said, "May almighty God have mercy on you, brethren! Did I not tell you that your manner of life and my own would not accord?" Having said this, he departed from the community and returned to the beloved solitude to resume his former eremitic life. But his fame continued steadily to increase, and his sanctity was plainly demonstrated by a multitude of signs and miracles. A vast number of people visited him, and many wished to join him in living the monastic life. And so within a short time, he had founded no less than twelve monasteries.

In one of these monasteries, there was a certain monk who found himself unable to stand still in prayer for any length of time. Rather, while the others were praying, he would leave the oratory and go and wander about outside. When the abbot of that monastery related this troubling thing to St. Benedict, he visited the monastery for himself, and saw the monk who was unable to remain still in prayer. And he noticed a small, black boy vexing the monk, pushing him about in a persistent fashion and drawing him to-and-fro by the cloth of his habit. Benedict was surprised at this uncanny thing, and said to the abbot and another monk,

Maur, "Do you not see the troublesome boy which is preventing this poor monk from standing still and causing him to wander around?" But both of them, perplexed, declared that they could see no such thing.

The saint then invited them to pray with him that they should be able to see the cause of the monk's strange behavior. And, behold, the eyes of Maur were opened and he perceived the small, impish boy. But the abbot of the monastery could still not see him.

The next day, Benedict found this monk outside wandering around aimlessly when he should have been in the oratory in prayer. With a certain degree of paternal severity and charitable discipline, he reprimanded him for his lack of wisdom and discernment and struck him with his staff. At this the monk fell down motionless. And after that the devil—for it was, in fact, the devil who had assumed the form of this vexatious child—never troubled him again. It was as if the staff of Benedict had not struck the hapless monk, but rather driven away the wicked tempter himself!

❁ ❁ ❁

Out of the dozen monasteries which Benedict founded, there were three which were located on the top of a rocky mountain. And each day, some monks of these communities would have to perform the laborious task of descending from the mountain, drawing water and carrying their burden back up to the mountain peaks. They often requested that Benedict would permit them to relocate their communities, so that they might be spared this arduous necessity.

So one night Benedict ascended the mountain, taking a young monk with him. There they prayed earnestly to God, and the saint positioned three large stones to identify a particular location amongst the mountainous peaks. The next morning, some of the brothers came to Benedict once more. This time, he said to them, "My sons, go to the very peak of the mountain, and on it you will find three large stones carefully positioned. At the spot marked by these stones, dig into the ground. And you will find that the Lord is able to produce for you all the water you need!"

So the brethren ascended the mountain and found the place where the three stones had been positioned. They began to dig in the place thus indicated, and suddenly crystal-clear water flowed forth! This water flowed continuously, forming a stream running from the peak of the mountain to its base. And this miraculous spring was sufficient to provide the monks with all the water they needed, and to spare them the irksome necessity of the daily trek down the mountain to visit the well.

In a certain place near one of St. Benedict's monasteries, one of the monks was engaged in clearing an area of land from the profusion of thornbushes and brambles which infested it. He was using an axe to do this, and it happened that the iron head of the axe he was using flew off the handle (such indeed was the vigor of his exertions!), and landed in a nearby pond. This pond was extremely deep, and the sunken axe head seemed to be irretrievably lost. The monk was, as may be imagined, overcome with anxiety and sorrow. But upon learning of this accident, blessed Benedict confidently took the handle of the axe and held it over the surface of the water. And immediately, the axe head sprung up from the depths of the pond and re-affixed itself to the handle!

One of St. Benedict's young disciples in the monastic life, a boy called Placid,[4] was once drawing water from a certain great river. Alas, whilst thus engaged the unfortunate neophyte slipped and fell into the deep and turbulent waters! Instantly the waves engulfed him and drew him out into the depths, until he was the distance of an arrow-shot from the bank. St. Benedict, the man of

4. According to ancient traditions, Placid was eight years of age when he joined St. Benedict's monastery. Like Benedict, he was of the illustrious Anicius family. A St. Placid (believed to be this same disciple of Benedict) is revered as a martyr in Sicily, where he founded a monastery. This monastery was attacked by Saracens and he, together with thirty other monks, were all slaughtered. See Usuard, *Martyrologium* (October 5), 542.

God, was back at the monastery in his cell when this occurred, but, through a spirit of prophecy, he knew immediately what had happened. At once he summoned another monk, Maur,[5] and related to him what had occurred, bidding him to set forth with all haste to rescue Placid from drowning. Having received a blessing from the saint, Maur rushed forth to the place where Placid had been drawing water. And so intent was he upon rescuing the lad that he did not halt even when he had arrived at the bank of the river, but continued running over the water just as if he was still running on the land! He found Placid, and grasping him by the hair, drew him forth from the waves and back to safety.

It was only after the rescue was complete that Maur realized the marvelous thing which had taken place. When he recounted it to Benedict, the saint humbly insisted that the miracle was not due to his own (Benedict's) merits or sanctity, but rather entirely attributable to the diligent and praiseworthy obedience of Maur himself.

There was a certain priest by the name of Florentius who became inflamed with envy at Benedict's reputation for holiness, and this envy soon grew into wicked malice. So Florentius took a loaf of bread, soaked it in poison and then took it to Benedict, pretending that he wished the saint to bless it for him and to accept it as a gift. Benedict took the bread gratefully, but sensing by prophetic insight that it was poisoned, gave it to a raven which he was in the habit of feeding. And he spoke to the bird thus, "In the name of the Lord Jesus Christ, take this bread to some place where no human shall ever find it!"

The raven then flew around the bread crowing vociferously, as if wishing to obey Benedict's instructions but somehow unable

5. St. Maur and St. Placid, the two disciples of Benedict mentioned by name in his life, entered monastic life on the same day in the year 523. According to tradition, St. Maur was sent to France by St. Benedict in 543, at the request of Innocentius, the bishop of Le Mans. He founded the first Benedictine monastery in France and served as its abbot, in a location now called St. Maur-sur-Loire.

to do so. The man of God then repeated his words, "I say to thee, my feathered friend, take thou this bread and hie thee hence with it! Then cast it away in some deserted place." Upon hearing this, the raven did exactly as it had been asked. After three days the sable-plumed fowl returned to the saint, to resume its wonted custom of accepting daily a little food from his venerable hand.

But despite the frustration of this attempted poisoning, the nefarious Florentius did not immediately cease his plotting against Benedict. For perceiving that he was unable to harm the body of the master, he resolved instead to attack the souls of his disciples. So he engaged seven beautiful maidens, and would pay them to go to the garden of the monastery and to play and dance there, quite naked.[6] It was, indeed, his scheme to incite thereby the young monks to thoughts of fornication and to inflame their hearts with the distracting and insidious fires of carnal lust.

When Benedict saw what was taking place and how Florentius was working to corrupt his community, he resolved to depart to another locality, together with his brethren monks. Now the dastardly Florentius was looking on as all of this was happening, sitting in a chamber at the top of a solarium (or sun-tower). And he rejoiced with a most wicked joy. Yet suddenly, the solarium collapsed and the envious cleric fell to his death!

Maur, who had remained behind and witnessed this, rushed after Benedict and the monks who were travelling with him. With great exultation, he said to him, "O master, the one who has been seeking to undermine you is now dead!" But the saint did not rejoice when he heard this, as one may well have expected him to do; but, on the contrary, he wept bitterly. Perhaps he wept to hear of the demise the Florentius himself; or perhaps he mourned that his disciple, Maur, should exult thus over the death of his foe.

Wisely, then, did Benedict enjoin Maur to repentance over his presumptuous exultation. He also declared that, though one

6. It is not entirely clear, either in the text of the *Legenda Aurea* or Gregory's *Life of Benedict,* whether the sending of these seductive dancers to the monastery was a once-off incident, or whether it was a regular practice of Florentius to do so. Benedict's decision to relocate the community seems to suggest the latter.

may change the location where one resides, nevertheless the real enemy—that is the devil—will work the same temptations in every place.

❁ ❁ ❁

In due course, Benedict moved to Monte Cassino and established a monastery there. He transformed an ancient temple of Apollo to a chapel dedicated to St. John the Baptist, and also converted the people of the area away from the practice of idolatry to the Christian faith.

This so infuriated the devil that he appeared before the eyes of the saint in a visible and most gruesome form, with acrid flames spewing forth from his eyes and mouth. He called upon the saint, saying "O Benedict! Benedict!" But when Benedict utterly ignored him and refused to respond, he cried out instead, "I should not call thee 'Benedict,' for that means 'blessed.' Rather I should dub thee, 'Accursed, accursed!' Why is it that thou doth persecute me thus?"[7]

❁ ❁ ❁

When the monastery at Monte Cassino was being constructed there was a large boulder which the monks needed to move for the purpose of their building work there. Yet, try as they might, they could not manage to budge the boulder, even when working together as a large group. But when the saint gave his blessing over the immense stone, instantly the boulder was moved without any effort at all! Reflecting upon this, he realized that it had been the devil himself who, until then, had been preventing them from shifting the boulder.

Another time, still in the days of the construction of the abbey at Monte Cassino, the monks were at work raising up a wall. And the devil again appeared to Benedict, and said to him maliciously, "I shall go off now to vex your beloved brethren!" But the saint hastily sent a message to the monks, urging them to exercise all

7. See Acts 9:4.

possible caution because the malign and cunning devil was intent upon causing them trouble.

Nevertheless, the devil did succeed in pushing the new wall over, and it fell upon a certain monk and crushed him to death. When the holy abbot heard of this, he ordered that the body of the unfortunate brother be placed in a sack and brought to him anon. This was done, and St. Benedict prayed over him. And, lo, the dead monk was instantly restored to full life and health!

THERE WAS A CERTAIN devout layman, who had a custom of visiting St. Benedict at his monastery once every year. And it was his practice to fast whilst making the journey there. But one year, another pilgrim joined him in his travels. This pilgrim had some food with him. Once evening had fallen, he said to his companion, "Come, brother, let us eat together, lest we lose strength for our journey." But the other explained that it was his intention to fast until he had completed his pilgrimage to visit the saint.

For the moment, his companion accepted his declining to share food with him with apparent good grace. But a little later, he asked him again to eat with him. And again, his companion politely refused. After they had travelled further and were both much fatigued, they came upon a cool fountain. The unknown pilgrim once more suggested to his companion that they should partake of the refreshment of a little food and drink. This time his companion gave in, and they ate together.

When the man finally reached the monastery at Monte Cassino, he was taken into the presence of St. Benedict. The saint looked upon him intently and said, "My son, the wicked devil tried to tempt you once, and was not able to succeed. Then he tried to tempt you a second time, and you successfully refused him. But when he tempted you for the third time, you were defeated!" Upon hearing this, the pilgrim realized that his mysterious travelling companion had, in fact, been the Prince of Darkness himself. Overcome with remorse, he fell at the feet of the holy abbot, and implored his prayers.

❁ ❁ ❁

Attila, the King of the Goths, wished to test whether or not St. Benedict really possessed the spirit of prophecy, as he was reputed to do. So he had a certain one of his officers dressed in his own royal robes and gave to him all the regalia and adornments of a king. He then sent him forth to the monastery, instructing the officer to pretend to be himself. But as soon as Benedict glanced at him, he saw through the attempted impersonation and said, "My son, discard this foolish disguise! For I perceive clearly that the costume you wear and the regalia that adorns your person is not, in sooth, your own at all."

And immediately, the officer fell to the ground, struck with awe and reverence, and deeply sorry that he had presumed to attempt to deceive such a sagacious and holy man.[8]

❁ ❁ ❁

There was a certain cleric who was greatly vexed by a devil. And he was taken to St. Benedict, in the hope that the man of God might be able to cure him of this affliction. The saint duly performed an exorcism. Once the man had been freed from the evil spirit that had hitherto vexed him, Benedict instructed him, "My son, henceforth eat no meat. And neither should you ever accept sacramental ordination to the priesthood. For if you are ever ordained as a priest, you will once more be delivered into the power of the wicked one!"

For a good while, the cleric carefully observed Benedict's injunctions. But as he saw many of his juniors being advanced to the priesthood, he became frustrated and envious. Eventually, casting Benedict's earnest warning to the desuetude of oblivion, he accepted the advancement which he felt was due to him, and was ordained as a priest. And from that time forth, the devil did indeed begin to vex and afflict him once more . . .

8. Caxton's Middle English version of this story states that the man fell down to the ground dead, but this is not the sense of either the *Legenda Aurea* version or Gregory's text.

❖ ❖ ❖

Once a certain man sent two flagons of wine to St. Benedict, through a servant of his. But this dishonest thrall hid one of the flagons along the way, and delivered only the other one. The man of God accepted this gift with expressions of gratitude. But—illuminated by the vision of prophecy which revealed to him the covert actions of all—he said to the servant, "My son, see to it that you don't drink from the other flagon, the one you have secretly hidden away for yourself! Rather, inspect it most cautiously to see what peril lurks therein!"

The servant was, naturally, deeply embarrassed and confused by this exposure of his own deceitfulness and attempted theft. Bearing in mind the words of the saint, when he came to the flagon which he had hidden, he looked inside cautiously. And there he found lurking within a deadly viper!

❖ ❖ ❖

There was a son of an illustrious and wealthy nobleman who had joined Benedict's monastery as a monk. On one occasion, he was assigned the duty of holding the lamp while Benedict ate his dinner. Alas, feelings of pride began to flare up in the young man's heart, and he secretly mused to himself, "Who am I that I should be reduced to standing here holding a lamp for this pitiful old man to eat his repast?"

As he was thinking thus, immediately the saint said to him, "Cross your heart, my son, cross your heart!" And, showing that he was capable of perceiving clearly the innermost sentiments of anyone's soul, he continued thus;

> "O, why, my son, doth there abide
> Within thy heart such wicked pride?
> Why despise, O haughty brother,
> The Love which bids us serve each other?"

And having said this, Benedict summoned another one of the brethren to himself, and handed him the lamp to hold. As for the proud monk, he gently directed him to go back to his cell and to reflect quietly on the sin of pride to which he had so easily succumbed . . .

❁ ❁ ❁

There was a certain chieftain of the Goths by the name of Galla, who was a member of the sect of the Arians.[9] He lived during the time of the aforementioned King Attila, and persecuted religious persons and the Catholic Church with a baleful ardor. Indeed, he once boasted that any cleric or monk who dared to appear before his face would not depart from him alive.

One day, goaded on by avarice, he captured a farmer and demanded of him all his money and treasures, beating the poor man mercilessly. But the farmer told him (quite truthfully) that he had given everything he possessed that was of value to St. Benedict, and had commended it all to his safe keeping. Upon hearing this, Galla ceased to beat him, but tied him by his arm to the bridle of his horse. He then compelled the farmer to lead him forth, so as to show him who this Benedict was and where he abided.

Thus the farmer led the brutal Goth to the saint's monastery. With the farmer still leading him, eventually Galla found Benedict, who was sitting alone in his cell and reading. The farmer said, "This is the holy Benedict of whom I spoke before." The barbarian was filled with fury and greed, and demanded of Benedict that he should at once hand over to him the money and treasures which the farmer had entrusted to him.

Upon hearing this, the saint raised his eyes and looked at both Galla and the captured farmer intently. He then turned his gaze to the ropes with which the farmer was bound. And at once these ropes began to unbind themselves, with a rapidity surpassing that which any human being could possibly achieve! The Goth was astounded and fell to the ground in awe, commending himself

9. The Arians were a heterodox Christian sect, who did not accept the consubstantiality of the Son and the Father, as affirmed in the Niceno-Constantinopolitan creed. At the time of Benedict, many of the Goths and other Germanic peoples still followed this sect.

to the prayers and mercy of the man of God, who could unbind strong ropes with a mere glance.

But Benedict continued his reading casually, barely raising his eyes from the book with which he was engaged. Finally, however, he warned the chieftain of the Goths to abandon his career of brutality, cruelty and tyranny. And henceforth, Galla never again engaged in the crimes of rapine, theft or intimidation, nor did he make any further efforts to oppress or persecute Catholics.

At one time a dire famine struck the Italian region of Campania. Lack of food afflicted the whole population, and even St. Benedict's monastery was totally bereft of supplies of grain. Their stores of bread were eventually so depleted that once when it was time for all the brethren to take their dinner, only five loaves could be found. When the holy abbot saw the monks looking dejected and depressed at this, he gently admonished them, saying, "Why are your hearts saddened by this lack of bread? Today we have little; but, by the grace of God, tomorrow we shall have an abundance!"

And it happened that, on the morn of the following day, some two hundred sacks filled with flour were discovered outside the cellar door! This was certainly the gracious gift of almighty God, but even to this day it remains an utter mystery as to how they came to be there . . .

When the brethren saw this wonder, they all gave heart-felt thanks to the Lord. Moreover, they learnt the valuable lesson that the generosity of Divine Providence is never to be doubted.

It is read that a certain man had a son who suffered from the grave and disfiguring malady known as "elephantiasis." This unfortunate youth was very badly afflicted by his rare disease. All his hair fell out, and he became progressively more and more swollen. And as he did so, the rumor of his grotesque condition spread far and wide throughout the land, fueled by the morbid and vulgar curiosity of the common people. Eventually he was sent to St. Benedict, who cured him promptly and completely by means of his prayers. The youth was filled with immense gratitude towards God, and dedicated the remainder of his life to good works.[10]

❁ ❁ ❁

Once St Benedict sent a group of monks to a certain location to construct a new monastery there. He also advised them that he would come to them on a particular day, in order to instruct them concerning the planning and arrangements of the new establishment. Now, on the night before he was due to visit them, he appeared in a dream to the monk who was in charge of the construction party. In this dream, he carefully indicated to that monk his desired layout for the monastery, and where the various buildings should be located.

But the next day, when this monk related his vision to the other monks, they all refused to put any trust or credence in the dream. And they were disappointed when Benedict did not appear in person, as he had promised them. So they all went back to the saint, and complained to him, "We waited for you patiently to come as you promised, Father Benedict. But you never arrived!"

The man of God responded, "Why ever do you say these things? Did I not appear to one of you in a dream, and clearly indicate how the monastery was to be arranged? Go forth, my sons, and complete the project just as I have instructed you." And having spoken thus, he dismissed the brothers to return to the site of their work and continue their assigned task there.

❁ ❁ ❁

Not far from Benedict's monastery, there was a convent of religious sisters. Within this community of nuns, there were two noblewomen who were both highly talkative and not at all able to restrain their tongues from gossip and chatter. Understandably,

10. Interestingly, this miracle is omitted entirely from Caxton's version of *The Golden Legend* (1483).

this undisciplined talk often provoked the superior of the community to anger and annoyance. So the superior related this problem to St. Benedict. He, in turn, sent a firm message to the talkative sisters, "Learn to restrain your speech, my sisters, or I shall have no choice but to exclude you both from holy communion!"

Yet, for various reasons, the superior did not pass this message on to them immediately. And, in just a few days, both of the talkative sisters died! Alas, neither of them had received Benedict's instruction on learning to restrain their speech before departing from this passing world. Following their deaths, according to custom, they were both duly buried in the church of the convent.

Now it happened soon afterwards that when Mass was being celebrated in that church, the deacon, pursuant to the usual ritual of the Mass, pronounced the instruction, "Whoever is not able to receive communion should now depart from the church." And, lo, the maidservant of the two deceased noblewomen saw them both arise from their tombs, stand up and walk out of the church!

Greatly disturbed by this, she reported her vision to St. Benedict. Upon hearing what she had seen, the saint gave to her an offering to present on behalf of the dead women, saying, "Go and offer this for their deceased souls, and then they shall no longer be excluded from communion, but gladly re-admitted!" This the maidservant did, presenting the offering Benedict had given her on behalf of the two women. And the next time Mass was celebrated in the church, she no longer saw the vision of the deceased nuns arising from their tombs to leave.

Once a monk of St. Benedict's monastery went to visit his parents, but he departed from the monastery without first receiving the saint's blessing. And it happened, alas, that on the very day he arrived to see them, he suddenly died.

But when they attempted to bury their deceased son, the ground opened up and rejected his body! This happened not only once, but a second and even a third time. The parents, greatly distressed, then went to see Benedict, and implored his blessing for their deceased son. The saint took a consecrated eucharistic host and handed it to them, saying "Place this upon his chest, and then lower him into the grave." The parents did this just as the holy abbot had instructed, and this time the body was accepted by the earth and buried successfully.

❁ ❁ ❁

There was another monk who, for various reasons, felt himself no longer able to remain in the monastery. He persistently requested of Benedict permission to depart from the community; and, eventually, the saint, much irritated and disappointed, granted him leave to do so.

But as he made his way from the monastery, he soon encountered a fierce dragon, standing before him on the road. The beast leered at him with gaping, voracious jaws and fetid, foul and fiery breath, and seemed fully intent upon devouring him. Aghast with fear, the horrified monk called out, "My brethren, run! Hasten hither and save my life, for this dragon is about to kill me!"

The brothers heard his cries, and they ran out to help him with all possible celerity. But they found no dragon there at all—just the monk, who was crouching and trembling with abject terror. They led him back to the monastery, and he promised henceforth never to attempt to leave again.

❁ ❁ ❁

There was another time when a severe famine again afflicted the region. During this time, St. Benedict would distribute all food and produce that was available to him to those who were destitute. Thus it came about that all the stores of the monastery were becoming drastically depleted, until nothing remained but a glass bottle filled with oil. And then the saint instructed the monk in charge of the cellar to give this one last bottle of oil to a certain needy person.

The cellarer heard this instruction, but he refused to obey it, lest the monks in the monastery should have nothing at all. When the man of God heard of this, he was infuriated. He ordered that the glass bottle of oil should be thrown out the window, so that no trace of disobedience should remain in the monastery.

This was done, and the glass vessel fell heavily upon a great rock on the ground below. But amazingly it was not broken, nor was a single drop of oil spilt! St. Benedict then ordered it to be taken up again, and given to the needy person, just as he had first instructed.

The cellarer-monk then sincerely reproved himself for his insubordination and lack of confidence in Divine Providence, praying earnestly to God for forgiveness. Now, there was a large stone flask in the monastery that had stood empty for some time. But after the remorseful monk had prayed, it was found to be full of oil! And it was not only full, but even overflowed its brim, so that abundant streams of fine oil flowed forth over the floor . . .

❁ ❁ ❁

On one occasion, Benedict went forth to visit his sister, Scholastica.[11] As they sat together at a table, she asked him if he would spend the night there, continuing their edifying and salubrious conversation until dawn. Benedict, however, would not by any means agree to this. She then bowed her head in prayer. And when she raised her head again, immediately tempestuous thunder and lightning began to resound, as well as an unremitting deluge of rain! Indeed, so torrential was the downfall that Benedict could not possibly set foot outside her dwelling that night—despite the fact that hitherto the weather had been perfectly fine.

Thus St. Scholastica, who poured out tears in her prayers, had transformed thereby the calm serenity of the sky into heavy rain.

11. According to ancient tradition, Scholastica, Benedict's sister, also lived a monastic life, in a community of nuns located close to her brother's monastery. Gregory's version of the narrative states that it was the custom of Benedict to visit his sister once each year for spiritual conversation. Other sources indicate that Scholastica was a twin to saint Benedict, and that she (like Benedict) had commenced her religious life as a hermit, before becoming the leader of a coenobium. Her feast is observed on February 10, the date on which she died.

Upon perceiving this marvel, the man of God exclaimed to her reprovingly, "My sister, what is this thing that you have done?"

To this his holy sibling replied;

"O Brother, I beseeched thee stay,
Yet thou, alas, didst answer 'Nay!'
But I then to the Lord did turn,
To grant the boon for which I yearn.

"Now God himself hath sent this rain,
Thy pious self here to detain,
That thus thou'll tarry through the night,
And we may talk till morning's light!"

To this, she added jestingly, "Leave me now, good brother, if thou be able!" But, of course, due to the violence of the tempest and heaviness of the rain, Benedict had no choice but to stay. Thus it transpired that the brother and sister spent the entire night together, engaged in the delights of holy colloquy on the spiritual life, celestial realities, and the wonders of Heaven.

It happened that just three days afterwards, when Benedict had returned to his monastery, he saw a vision of the soul of his beloved sister ascending into Heaven in the form of a radiant, white dove. And, indeed it was found to be the case that Scholastica had then died. Benedict ordered her body to be taken to his own monastery at Monte Cassino, and buried there in the same tomb which he had made ready for himself.

❁ ❁ ❁

Shortly after this, one night as the servant of God, Benedict, was gazing out through the window of his cell in prayer, he perceived a brilliant ray of light shining down through the pitchy opacity of the starless skies. And suddenly it was as if he could see the whole world—or rather, the whole created cosmos—contained within the pellucid effulgence of that single glowing beam!

And amongst the revelations contained within that glorious ray of light, he saw the soul of Germanus, the bishop of Capua, ascending into Heaven. And, indeed, later he was to learn that this same Germanus had, in fact, passed away at that very time.

During that same year, he foretold his own demise to several of the brothers. Precisely six days before his death, he ordered the tomb which he had prepared as his final resting place to be opened. Then he began to suffer from a fever, which grew steadily more severe each day. When the sixth day had arrived, he requested that he should be taken to the oratory. There he was fortified by receiving the sacrament of the Body and Blood of the Lord. Supported by the hands of his disciples, the saint stood upright with his eyes raised longingly to Heaven. And with words of suppliant prayer, he gave forth his noble spirit unto God as he breathed his last.[12]

Now on the same day on which the man of God had left this terrestrial realm and passed over to Christ, two monks received precisely the same revelation. These two brethren were in locations far removed from each other—one was alone in his cell, while the other was some considerable distance from the monastery. Both saw a glowing and luminous pathway, strewn with cloth-of-gold and innumerable, radiant lamps. This led from the cell of St. Benedict upwards to the Heavens.

And a certain man of venerable appearance appeared before them, and asked the monks, "To whom does this pathway belong?" When each of the monks confessed that they did not know, the man said to them, "This is the pathway prepared for St. Benedict, by which that noble servant of God even now ascends to the glory of Heaven!"

Benedict was buried in the oratory of St. John the Baptist at Monte Cassino, at the place where there had formerly been a temple of Apollo which the saint had destroyed. He died in the year of our Lord 518,[13] under the reign of the Emperor Justin I.

12. According to ancient traditions, the day on which Benedict died was March 21, and a Holy Saturday, i.e. the day before Easter Sunday. It was then about forty days after he had spent the night in holy conversation with his sisters, Scholastica.

13. Most scholars today believe that Benedict died in about 547.

Let us pray devoutly that St. Benedict may intercede to the Lord for us, so that we may have grace after this life to come to everlasting bliss in Heaven! Amen.[14]

14. This short concluding prayer is not found in the original Latin text, but appears in Caxton's Middle English version.

2

The Tale of the Relocation of the Bodies of St. Benedict and St. Scholastica into France

BY ADREVALD,

A MONK OF FLEURY

(C.820–879)

i. The Lombards invade Italy and suppress the monastery at Monte Cassino

In the dark and distant days of yore,[1] the fierce people of the Lombards[2] preferred to wallow, benighted, in the murky shadows of error and superstition, rather than to be illuminated by the resplendent light of the eternal truth. And they not only refused to accept the noble Christian faith themselves, but also sought to deter other peoples from its practice—by violence and by intimidation, by fire and by sword. Thus it was that they resolved to invade the land of Italy, both to overturn Christianity there and to subdue the Italian people to their own oppressive dominion. And, for reasons known only to the unseen judgment of God, Divine Providence permitted the Italian people to be conquered by these fearsome Lombards and to be subjugated to the imperious and truculent spears of the barbarian invaders.

The Lombards made bloody incursions throughout the entire expanse of Italy, and, in due course, attacked the beautiful province of Benevento.[3] Rabid indeed were their onslaughts and merciless their attacks! For they razed many of its cities to the ground, depopulated its monasteries and villages, and put to the sword a multitude of the Christian faithful. Attacking the flock of Christ as ravenous wolves attack sheep, they overturned many of the sheepfolds of this gentle flock of the faithful, destroying innumerable churches, shrines and holy places. Thus it was that the province of Benevento, which had previously been a verdant and tranquil pasture for the sheep of Christ became, as it were, a barren desert and a desolate wasteland.

Amongst such egregious works of depredation, the Lombards laid to waste the great and venerable monastery of our holy father St. Benedict, located at Monte Cassino. Its monks were expelled,

1. That is, in the late sixth century.

2. The Lombards were a Germanic people, who dominated much of Italy from the sixth to the eight centuries. Their name in Latin ("*langobardi*") means "long-beards."

3. A province in the Italian region of Campania.

and the monastery itself was left as a deserted ruin. Those who have carefully read the *Dialogues* of Gregory the Great will find that this tragic occurrence was, in fact, foretold by Benedict himself, in a moment of divine prescience. For he, imbued with a spirit of prophecy, had predicted that the monastery at Monte Cassino would be overturned and abandoned shortly after his death.[4]

4. See *Translator's Introduction*.

ii. Leodebodus founds the monastery at Fleury in France, supported by King Clovis II

After this devastation had occurred, many years passed. The site of the monastery at Monte Cassino which had once been the beloved home to a multitude of holy monks now became a dwelling place for wild beasts, ravens and owls. This deplorable situation continued even until the time when Clovis II, the son of Dagobert I, became King of France.[5] This King Clovis excelled in all virtues, and governed his kingdom with the utmost prudence and circumspection. Moreover, like a true Christian monarch, he was always eager to respond positively and encouragingly to whatever just requests and entreaties were made to him by those who served the Lord.

Thus it came to pass that Leodebodus, the abbot of the monastery of St. Anian in the French region of Orleans, humbly asked the king to agree to sell to him a certain piece of land known as Fleury, not far from the banks of the Loire River. It was his pious intention to found a Benedictine monastery there, for he had recently inherited a large sum of money following the death of his parents, and was keen to use these funds to establish a new monastic community. The field of Fleury (which means "filled with flowers") was then in the king's possession. The pious monarch was delighted to hear of the plan to found a monastery there, and gladly agreed to sell the property to Leodebodus for a most reasonable sum. For those who are curious, the original contract of this exchange is preserved to this very day in the archives of our monastery.[6]

Once the transaction had been finalized, Leodebodus set about fulfilling what he had planned to do with admirable alacrity and indefatigable industriousness. He began by having buildings suitable for a monastic community constructed at Fleury. To this endeavor he applied himself with wisdom and determination, which soon bore visible fruit. As well as buildings to accommodate

5. In about 639.

6. That is, Fleury Abbey.

monks, a basilica dedicated to St. Peter was raised up, and then another in honor of the Virgin Mary, the holy Mother of God.

Once the construction was complete, lest it should prove to be merely a useless folly and become a proverbial "monastery without monks," he recruited many young men who felt called to offer their service to God, through the monastic life of prayer, contemplation and fraternal charity. And he appointed a faithful and trustworthy man called Mummolus to serve as father and abbot to the newly-founded community, and to lead them in accordance with the Gospel and the holy Rule of St. Benedict.

iii. Aigulf is sent to Monte Cassino by Mummolus to recover the mortal remains of St. Benedict

With the passing of time, Leodebodus, the founder of the monastery at Fleury, went the way of all mortal flesh and departed from this earthly valley of tears. And we confidently believe that, on account of his holy life, he was granted admittance to the Kingdom of eternal peace and joy amongst the saints and angels in Heaven. Mummolus continued to serve as abbot at the monastery at Fleury, and did this with such talent and dedication that the community there grew and flourished.

It happened that one day, when Mummolus was earnestly perusing the writings of that most illustrious and learned Roman pontiff, St. Gregory the Great, he chanced to read how St. Benedict had ended his days in the monastery at Monte Cassino. He also read how, before his death, Benedict had predicted that this same monastery would be captured and overturned by barbarian invaders. Furthermore, the author, Gregory, averred that he had witnessed this sad prophecy being fulfilled with his own eyes.

After reading this, and acting upon the inspiration of the Holy Spirit, Mummolus resolved to send one of his monks to visit the location of the abandoned monastery at Monte Cassino, in the hope of recovering the body of St. Benedict from its ruins. Mummolus had, in fact, received a vision from Heaven that this was destined to happen, and in accordance with the will of God.

So he chose for this purpose a trustworthy brother called Aigulf. Aigulf was a dauntless and devout monk, distinguished for virtue, courage and sanctity, as the events which follow amply testify. Indeed, this Aigulf was, in the end, to earn the glorious crown of martyrdom, giving up his life for the sake of his faith.[7]

7. Aigulf, who is venerated as a saint, was later to become abbot of the Lérins Monastery on the island of Saint-Honorat in the French riviera. This monastery fell victim to violent attacks from Saracen raiders, and Aigulf himself died there as a martyr. The same Adrevald of Fleury who wrote this history also composed a biography St. Aigulf. See Adrevald, *Vita Sancti Aigulfi*.

iv. Some monks at the monastery at Le Mans receive a vision instructing them to find the tomb of St. Scholastica

At about the same time, it happened that certain monks at the monastery at Le Mans[8] also received a vision, which proved to be miraculously consistent with that of Mommolus. For in this vision, they saw themselves travelling to the region of Monte Cassino, and there recovering the body of St. Scholastica, Benedict's holy sister. It was shown to them also that the bodies of both saints, Benedict and Scholastica, rested in the same tomb in that location.

The monks who saw this vision were by no means hesitant or indolent in seeking to carry out what had been revealed to them, for they sensed that it was a genuine message from God. After a few days of preparation, those who had experienced this revelation departed from the monastery at Le Mans, and commenced the long journey southwards to Monte Cassino.

These monks stopped along the way at the monastery at Fleury, to take some much-needed respite from their travels. When they arrived there, they soon learned that Aigulf was also about to embark on a journey for Italy. For at that time, Aigulf, who had been chosen for this mission, had not yet set out upon his way.

Now, at this point the monks from Le Mans did not know the purpose of Aigulf's intended journey; nor, for that matter, did he know what their purpose was in travelling to Italy, either. Little did they suspect that, by some unknown serendipity, they shared a common destination and common purpose!

Nevertheless (despite the fact that they were not cognizant of the fact that they shared the same goal), in a spirit of monastic fraternity they resolved to make their journey together, pledging not to be separated until they had crossed the hallowed threshold of St. Peter's Basilica in Rome.

8. About 115 miles west of Paris.

v. The party of monks arrives in Rome together, but then Aigulf ventures forth alone to Monte Cassino and receives there a mysterious vision

After a long and arduous journey, the intrepid party—comprising the monks of Le Mans together with Aigulf of Fleury—arrived safely in the great city of Rome. There they entered the Basilica of St. Peter together, and all prayed earnestly for the success of their respective missions.

But the pledge they had made not to be separated until after they had entered that great basilica proved to have been prophetic, for shortly afterwards, a disagreement sprang up amongst them. Whereas Aigulf was eager to continue to Monte Cassino without delay to search for St. Benedict's tomb, his companions wished to spend some time in Rome first, visiting its various sacred sites, before continuing with their business. So they parted company, and Aigulf set out alone to Monte Cassino.

When Aigulf had arrived in that locality, he took lodgings in a certain village there. Yet, though he knew that Benedict's tomb must be somewhere in the area, he had no idea of its precise location. So he directed his prayers and entreaties to God, beseeching him to send him some sign or omen by which he might be able to find the saint's resting place.

After this, Aigulf sat himself down in the village, casting his eyes all around him for some sign which might direct him to St. Benedict's tomb. And he suddenly saw a certain man, apparently of very great age. This old man looked at Aigulf curiously, and asked him, "Who are you, my lad, and what brings you to these parts?" But the monk did not dare to disclose his business—which was certainly something out of the ordinary—to this inquisitive stranger. Nevertheless, the old man persisted in his enquiries. "Why not share with me your secrets?" said he. "Do not fear that I should betray your trust in me, for you shall find that I know well how to keep a secret. Furthermore, if you tell me what is your purpose in coming here—who knows?—perhaps I can help you bring it to fruition!"

The servant of God, Aigulf, listened to these words attentively, and considered that it is often the elderly who possess the most accurate knowledge of past events. Moreover, it could be (so he thought) that the Lord himself had brought this old man to him in answer to his prayers. So he proceeded to relate to him the reason for his coming to Monte Cassino, and his hopes of discovering the tomb of St. Benedict. To this, the old man replied, "If you agree to offer me suitable recompense for my help, I can indeed assist you so that you will very soon accomplish that which you mean to do."

Upon hearing these words, Aigulf was greatly encouraged. "Please be assured," quoth he, "that there will be no problem in paying you handsomely for your services!"

The old man then said, "When night falls and darkness descends upon the earth this evening, tarry not in bed, but arise and climb up onto the roof of your dwelling place. Then look forth to the hills and cast your eyes to the wilderness. And you shall behold there a bright light, glowing with all the radiance of a snow-capped mountain. My son, note well the location which this light illuminates! For there it is that you shall find the treasure for which you seek."

And, having said this, the mysterious old man vanished into thin air . . . .

vi. Aigulf finds the ancient tomb, and he, together with the monks from Le Mans, take the remains of the two saints back to France

Placing his confidence in the counsel of the old man whom he saw in his vision, that evening Aigulf roused himself from his bed during the first watch of the night, and ascended to the roof of the inn where he was staying. Looking upon the deserted hills which surrounded the village, he saw a radiant light, like a glowing cloud, hovering above a certain location. Upon beholding this, he was filled with both astonishment and joy. How fervently he praised and blessed the King of the universe and the Monarch of the ages for his most gracious providence! And, having carefully noted the place illuminated by the light, he spent the remainder of the night offering praise and thanks to God.

The next morning, as soon as the golden orb of the sun had arisen in the east, he set forth on foot until he reached the exact location above which the glowing cloud had hovered the night before. And there he found an ancient stone chest or sarcophagus. The sarcophagus was dirty, crude and dilapidated in its exterior aspect, but what precious treasures were contained within it! For here, truly, were two "pearls of great price"[9]—the mortal remains of the holy brother and sister, St. Benedict and St. Scholastica.

Examining the sarcophagus carefully, Aigulf found upon it etched a timeworn but still legible inscription, confirming this indeed to be the tomb of the saints. Carefully opening the tomb, he found within it a single casket containing the sacred bones of both.

But at this point, the monks from Le Mans, from whom he had been separated in Rome, suddenly arrived on the scene. For, since Aigulf had parted company with them, they had likewise continued on their quest to locate the tomb of St. Scholastica. And it was only at this point, now that they had all discovered the location of the tomb, that they revealed to each other the secret purpose of their respective missions—for Aigulf, to find the body of

9. See Matt 13:45–46.

Benedict, and for the monks from Le Mans, to recover the mortal remains of Scholastica.

After much rejoicing and thanking God for his kindness in guiding them to the goal of their quests, Aigulf and the other monks carefully removed the casket containing the two saints. They then commenced the long journey northwards, back to their homeland of France.

vii. The pope sends officers to pursue Aigulf and his companions, but they escape safely, thanks to the assistance of Heaven

Making good pace in their travels, Aigulf and the monks of Le Mans soon approached the borders of France. But as they took their rest one night, they heard a thunderous voice from Heaven. It spoke with authority and power, saying, "Make no delay! Hasten upon your way, lest you be overtaken and captured by those who would prevent your return to your native land!"

Now, at precisely the same time in Rome, the pope himself was taking his rest within his splendid bedchamber.[10] But he suddenly awoke, and he also heard a voice from Heaven. It spoke to him in tones of reproach; "Why do you take your ease and lie here on your bed, when you should be taking care of the region entrusted to you? Why do you neglect what is useful for the people of Italy and worry only about your own concerns? For you, at this very moment, are being deprived of the patronage and protection of the noble Benedict and his sister Scholastica, who lie buried hereabouts. For foreigners have come and discovered their remains, and even now are carrying them off to a distant land!"

Having been thus alerted, the pontiff summoned to himself his officers. He related to them the revelation he had received, and ordered them to go forth in pursuit of the foreigners who had discovered the remains of Benedict and Scholastica and were taking them away from the soil of Italy. These officers of the pope then went forth to find and capture Aigulf and his companions, and recruited some of the Lombard warriors to support them in their pursuit.

But Aigulf and the monks of Le Mans, having been warned by a divine vision, hastened on their way. For they realized that they were being pursued by those who sought to prevent them from bringing the remains of Benedict and Scholastica to France.

10. The pope in question is not identified here by name. Clearly, he must have been one of the popes between the times of Gregory I and Gregory II. There were some twenty-four popes during this period of approximately a hundred years.

Aigulf turned to the Lord in prayer, and implored his assistance in bringing about their escape.

And God, the omnipotent King, responded favorably to this humble request. For a dense and opaque darkness enshrouded Aigulf and his companions, so that they were rendered totally invisible to their pursuers, though they could see their own way forward. And thus it was that Aigulf, the servant of Christ, and his companions, were able to escape from the officers of the pope and continue on their way to France, bearing with them the precious mortal remains of the two great saints.

viii. Various miracles occur during their journey

They made steady progress on their journey, passing through a great many regions and villages as they did so. And it happened that they reached a certain village called Bonnée in the French province of Orleans.[11] There Aigulf, together with the monks from Le Mans, stopped for a few days, taking respite from the fatigue of their travels.

Now, there was a certain man in this village who had been born blind. When he learned that the party of pilgrim-monks were bearing with them the holy remains of the great St. Benedict, he at once sought them out. Falling to his knees, he prayed with fervor and faith that, through the merits of St. Benedict, God would vouchsafe to him the gift of vision, which nature had so cruelly denied him. And—behold!—within the space of a single hour, he had gained the faculty of perfect sight. How boundless was his joyful astonishment and how ecstatic his gratitude as he rendered thanks to God and St. Benedict for their mercy and kindness to him!

And, lo, it pleased the Divinity to make another manifestation of power and benevolence in that same location. For there was also there a crippled man, whose limbs were so badly shriveled and feeble that he could neither walk nor stand upright, but rather was compelled to crawl along the ground to move about. He also came to Aigulf and his companions, and implored the assistance of God, through the intercession and merits of St. Benedict. Once he had completed this earnest prayer, a remarkable transformation began to take place in the man's body. For his contorted and shriveled limbs seemed to fill with blood and vitality, and the nerves which controlled his movements gradually became fully animated. Within a short space of time, he was able to stand fully erect and to move about freely—a veritable picture of health, life and vigor!

All the citizens of Bonnée came to know of these miraculous healings, and blessed St. Benedict with the greatest joy and gratitude. And as a memorial to these wonderful events, they raised

11. Bonnée is about a league away from the Abbey at Fleury.

up a basilica dedicated to the holy patriarch, which stands in that town to this very day.

When the party departed from Bonnée, they next went through a village called *La Maririe de Neuville,* situated only about five miles from the monastery at Fleury. They decided to rest their feet for a little while in that area. But a blind man of the village came to know of their presence, and rushed out to meet them. And with passionate eagerness, he forcibly seized from them the basket containing the precious relics of St. Benedict!

When Aigulf, the servant of the Lord, endeavored to correct the man with pious admonitions, he adamantly refused to give the basket back. "Never shall I return these relics to you," quoth he with firm resolve, "until God, through the merits of St. Benedict, returns to me my vision! For I know full well that, such was the faithfulness of this holy thaumaturge Benedict, that whatever he asks of the Lord will most assuredly be granted."

And—behold!—his sight was restored to him at that very instant. With infinite gratitude and reverence, he returned the basket containing the saint's mortal remains to the hands of its rightful custodians.

ix. In the town of Old Fleury, citizens from Le Mans demand of Aigulf the body of St. Scholastica, to which he eventually agrees

It was not very long before all the people, both clergy and laity, who inhabited the area came to hear of the return of Aigulf and his companion monks from the expedition to Italy; they heard, too, of the fact that they carried with them the priceless remains of St. Benedict and his holy sister, St. Scholastica. And so, with great jubilation, an enthusiastic crowd assembled to greet them. They met them in the township known as "Old Fleury," not very far from the Fleury monastery. This was on the eleventh day of the month of July, and the bodies of the saints were received with the utmost solemnity and joy, and then reverently installed in the local church.[12]

But it happened that some citizens of Le Mans heard of this. The reader will recall that a number of monks from the monastery at that city had accompanied Aigulf on his journey to Italy, in the hope of obtaining the holy relics of the body of St. Scholastica. Accordingly, they earnestly requested Aigulf that he should now permit them to take the remains of Scholastica with them back to Le Mans, in fulfilment of what had been divinely revealed to a number of their monks in a dream.

However, Aigulf was hesitant to consent to this request. "Never should the bodies of this brother and sister be separated!" he protested. "For just as they were buried together in their previous resting place, so ought they now also be housed together." But certain of the more prudent and prominent citizens disagreed with Aigulf's resolution, and attempted to change his mind. They pointed out that the monks from Le Mans were acting upon a divine inspiration, which could not be ignored or contradicted; and that, moreover, they had shared in all the labor and peril of the expedition, and should not be deprived of its benefits. Furthermore, the

12. This day, July 11, is traditionally observed as the "Feast of the Translation of St. Benedict." In the current Roman church calendar, the feast of St. Benedict is now observed on that date.

remains of both St. Benedict and St. Scholastica were each of such great significance and power (they said) that it was wrong and presumptuous for a single place to possess both treasures, when the remains of one alone would more than suffice to sanctify and bless it adequately.

In the end, Aigulf was convinced, and humbly allowed himself to be persuaded by these sound arguments and wise counsels. He decided, therefore, to retain the holy relics of St. Benedict with himself to be taken to Fleury Abbey, whilst permitting the companions of his quest—the monks from Le Mans—to take the venerable body of St. Scholastica with them back to their own city.

x. The bones of St. Benedict and St. Scholastica are successfully separated, and two dead persons are restored to life

However, it soon became clear that it was going to be no easy matter to separate the remains of Benedict from those of Scholastica. For the holy brother and sister had been entombed in a single casket, and then transported together in a single basket. Thus the bones were all mixed together, in a large and utterly confused pile. Aigulf and the others were perplexed and uncertain about how to proceed. One of the party suggested that they should simply separate the larger bones from the smaller ones, assuming the former to belong to Benedict and the latter to come from Scholastica. This was done, and the bones were arranged into two collections, one of larger bones and one of smaller bones. However, no-one was entirely satisfied that this was a reliable and sure way of determining whose bones were whose. And so the problem remained unsolved, and apparently unsolvable.

At this point, Aigulf and the monks from Le Mans decided that it was best to resort to the Lord, in the hope that God might send them some providential sign to assure them that they had separated the bones accurately. And so they spent the entire night in a vigil of prayer—and not the monks only, but also a multitude of the townspeople.

After the sun had arisen and the prayer vigil concluded, the attention of the monks fell upon two bodies which were then in the church. One was of a recently deceased young man, and the other of a recently deceased young woman; both, indeed, were due to be buried that day.

Inspired by the Holy Spirit, Aigulf ordered that the body of the young man should be placed near the place where the larger bones had been arranged, and brought into contact with them. [He did this in the hope that God would provide some visible sign, confirming that this group of bones were really those of Benedict.] And immediately when the corpse of the young man was brought into contact with the bones of Benedict, a most miraculous thing happened. For the body resumed its color and animation, and the man opened his eyes, fully alive!

Filled with joy and astonishment, they then brought the body of the young woman to the collection of smaller bones, likewise bringing her corpse into contact with them. And the same marvelous thing occurred, the girl being immediately restored to life! And so her family and friends, who had brought her to the church the previous day, dead, with much mourning and weeping, now took her home, alive and well, all filled with unspeakable joy and exultation.

[By these wonderful events, Aigulf and the other monks were assured that they had separated the bones of Benedict and Scholastica accurately.] And God also thereby confirmed that Benedict and Scholastica were truly brother and sister. For just as they (as twins) had been generated through a single act of procreation, so they now showed themselves to be twins also in sanctity and power, each procuring the same variety of miracle at the same place and on the same occasion.

This astonishing work of bringing the dead back to life calls to mind the miracle of Elijah in the days of long ago, [in which he had raised up a deceased boy.][13] Through this occurrence, God showed Benedict to equal the ancient patriarchs and prophets in holiness and virtue. And the words of the voice of divine truth were also fulfilled, in which Christ declared that, "Whoever believes in me shall perform the same deeds which I have performed."[14] All those who were present on that day and who had witnessed what transpired praised the Lord with the deepest awe and reverence—not only for restoring the young man and young woman to life, but also for using this miracle to confirm the identity of the bones of St. Benedict and St. Scholastica.

13. See 1 Kgs 17:21–22.

14. John 10:12.

xi. The remains of St. Scholastica are installed in a church at Le Mans, and a convent of nuns is established there

With all possible doubt about the identity of the holy relics of the saints now removed and any uncertainty concerning the separation and sorting of their bones now resolved, the monks and citizens of Le Man took possession of the remains of St. Scholastica with the greatest joy. And with care and reverence they bore this precious treasure back to their own city.

A magnificent church, adorned with the most sumptuous splendor, was raised up by the citizens of Le Mans to house in a fitting style the bones of St. Scholastica.[15] A convent of nuns, dedicated to the saint, was also very soon founded. And many noble women joined this community, inspired by the example of Scholastica to exchange their worldly wealth and status for the greater glory of serving the Lord. This holy convent has, until the present time, been rendered illustrious by the Lord with countless miracles and wonders.

15. St. Scholastica is today revered as the patron saint of the diocese and city of Le Mans. It is believed that most of her remains were seized by Norman raiders in the ninth century, and that the remaining relics were destroyed by fire in the twelfth century.

xii. The remains of St. Benedict are reverently installed at Fleury, accompanied by wondrous signs

Meanwhile, the bones of St. Benedict were finally taken to the monastery at Fleury. There Mummolus, the abbot, and Aigulf reverently placed them in the church dedicated to St. Peter.[16] They continued to deliberate, however, on the most fitting final resting place for these hallowed remains within the monastery complex, and conferred with the members of the monastic community on this matter. And there was much diversity of opinion and uncertainty concerning the question.

But it was not long before God, in his divine mercy, provided a visible sign whereby he made manifest the precise location which he had decreed as the resting place for the mortal remains of his honored servant, Benedict. For one night Abbot Mummolus was lying sleepless in bed, turning over in his mind the issue of where to bury Benedict's bones. He quietly arose from his bed and went out of the dormitory to walk out in the open, hoping that the sight of the night sky might provide him with some inspiration, or at least relief from his anxious deliberations. And God, who always gives ear to the just petitions of his servants, did not fail to hear the prayers of Mummolus, nor to offer him a visible response. For—behold!—suddenly a radiant light shone down from Heaven, like a flaming torch. Its aureate coruscations illuminated distinctly a particular location just before the church dedicated to the Virgin Mary, expressing very clearly that it was that place, and no other, that God had chosen as the earthly resting place for the holy relics of St. Benedict.

How relieved and overjoyed was Mummolus to receive this sign from Heaven! All his doubts and uncertainties were at once dispelled. An ornate and splendid shrine was constructed, and on the fourth day of December the bones of Benedict were installed

16. As mentioned in chapter 2, two churches had been constructed at the newly established Fleury Abbey, one dedicated to St. Peter and one dedicated to the Virgin Mary. The church dedicated to St. Peter, mentioned here, is no longer in existence.

there, accompanied by heart-felt divine praises and the greatest possible solemnity, honor and jubilation.[17] Thus the saint's remains were committed to the earth—a celestial treasure of inestimable value enclosed within the humble casement of a small urn.

Indeed, the multitude of miracles which have occurred in the presence of those holy relics testifies powerfully to just how dearly they are loved by God! For there have been innumerable cures of those sick in body, and even more healings of those afflicted by torments and maladies of the soul. And these have continued without ceasing until this very day.

But the biography of the saint himself provides evidence of the singular nobility and sanctity of the place in Fleury where his remains rest. For it is recorded that, towards the end of his life, Benedict beheld a brilliant ray of light shining from Heaven, and perceived the whole world mystically contained within that single ray of supernal light. It is not to be doubted that this ray illuminated the place of his future rest, and that the saint loved that special place beyond any other location in the entire world, and therefore desired most earnestly that his bones should abide there.[18]

And if all the miracles which have occurred in that place at Fleury Abbey where the bones of the holy patriarch St. Benedict

17. A feast of the Burial of St. Benedict continued to be observed in the region of Orleans on December 4 until about the eleventh century.

18. This is a reference to an incident recorded in St. Gregory's *Life of Benedict* (chapter 35), in which it is said that towards the end of his life Benedict saw a ray of light from Heaven, and perceived the whole world to be contained within that light. The incident is related thus: "The man of God, Benedict, being diligent in keeping vigils, rose early up before morning prayer (his monks being still at rest) and came to the window of his chamber, where he offered up his prayers to almighty God. Standing there, all of a sudden in the dead of the night, he saw a brilliant light, which banished away the darkness of the night, and glittered with such brightness, that the light which shone in the midst of darkness was far brighter than the light of the day. And then an astonishing miracle followed; for, as he himself did relate, the whole world was presented before his eyes, united in the single beam of light." The implication in the present text seems to be that the ray of light was directed towards the location of the future Fleury Abbey, where (according to this account) his bones would be interred. The same incident is related in somewhat abbreviated form in the *Legenda Aurea* version of Benedict's life, included in this volume.

rest were to be recorded in writing, the entire world would not be large enough to hold all the books which would need to be written![19] Amen.

19. See John 21:25.

3

The History of the Discovery of the Bodies of St. Benedict and St. Scholastica at Monte Cassino

BY PETER THE DEACON,
A MONK AND LIBRARIAN TO THE MONASTERY
AT MONTE CASSINO

(C.1115–1159)

i. The discovery of the tomb of St. Benedict and St. Scholastica

In about the year of our Lord 1150, upon the evening before the Octave of the Feast of St. Benedict,[1] *Peter the Deacon, a monk at the monastery at Monte Cassino and the librarian to the same venerable community, addressed the assembled monks. He spoke to them thus:*

My beloved brethren! Tomorrow we observe the Octave of the Feast of our most revered father and founder, St. Benedict, and we shall celebrate also the rediscovery of the holy remains of that most blessed man at our own beloved abbey of Monte Cassino. Therefore it is truly fitting that we should rejoice and exult, and that we all be filled with the joy of Christ himself and of the glorious saints and angels. And it is those who enjoy not only the outward festivities and feasting of these auspicious days but who also sincerely exult in the inner depths of their minds and hearts, who celebrate in a most worthy manner.

My brother monks, it seems appropriate on this night for me to relate to you the astounding events pertaining to the discovery of the tomb and body of St. Benedict, so that no one may have reason to doubt or to be uncertain of what it actually is which we will be celebrating tomorrow. These events took place in the days when the great Abbot Desiderius led our monastic community, almost a century ago now.[2]

At that time, Desiderius was undertaking extensive renovations of the crypt of our venerable church, dedicated to St. John the Baptist, which was then in a state of some disrepair. Now, on the very same date as it shall be tomorrow—that is, the eighth day after the Feast of St. Benedict—some of the monks were digging within the crypt of the church, removing the soil and debris which had accumulated there over the centuries. After they had dug down

1. The "Octave of the Feast of St. Benedict" refers to a kind of renewed celebration customarily held eight days after the major feast day.

2. Desiderius was abbot of Monte Cassino from about 1058 to 1086. Following this, he was elected to the papacy. He assumed his reign (as Pope Victor III) in 1086, and died about a year later.

about three feet, they came across a very old and mysterious tomb. Carefully reading the inscription carved into its ancient stone, they discovered that it contained within it a priceless treasure, for it was the tomb of none other than St. Benedict himself, as well as his holy sister, St. Scholastica!

What merriment did then resound
Because that ancient tomb was found;
What happiness did fill each mind
At this sacred, hallowed find;

Yea, that the bones in earth concealed
Were at last to sight revealed,
And that such relics, long unknown,
Should to mortal eyes be shown!

❁ ❁ ❁

BUT IT WAS NOT only their hearts which trembled and quaked with astonishment at the discovery. For the mountain itself, the great Monte Cassino, shook also from its very base! Indeed, earthquakes were reported in seventeen different nearby locations that day, as well as at the monastery itself. And a fragrance of heavenly sanctity and serenity began to emanate from the tomb of the saints. It filled the entire church with an indescribable sweetness, which brought ineffable delight and serenity to the souls of all who smelled it.

Furthermore, at the time when the tomb of holy Benedict was unearthed, it is attested that a number of miraculous healings also occurred in the district. There was a certain peasant living nearby, who had become possessed by some evil spirit. Once the venerable tomb was found and uncovered, this possessed man began to cry out. He (or rather, the wicked spirit within him) exclaimed in a voice both strident and lugubrious, "Alas, St. Benedict is driving us out! Alas, St. Benedict is driving us out!" He repeated this many times, then collapsed to the ground, utterly still and as if struck dead. But a little while later he returned to consciousness, and was found to be restored to perfect sanity.

There was another man who also suffered from attacks from malign spirits, from the city of Bari,[3] who was staying at the monastery at that time in order to benefit from the prayers of the monks. And he likewise was cured at precisely the same moment as the tomb was found.

The monks all rejoiced greatly that day, not only on account of the discovery of the priceless treasure of St. Benedict's tomb, but at the wondrous marvels worked by God. Indeed, these miracles served as irrefutable evidence of the authenticity of the discovery, confirming that the tomb really did contain the mortal remains of the great saint.

❁ ❁ ❁

As that auspicious day drew to its close and twilight fell, several brothers were appointed by Abbot Desiderius to keep a watchful vigil at the tomb for the entire night. Once these monks had assembled for this duty, the warden of the church, a monk called Giorgio, said to them, "Brothers, why don't we have a quick look at the relics within this tomb before Abbot Desiderius arrives?" Indeed, all the brethren were filled with the utmost eagerness and curiosity, so this suggestion pleased them greatly and met with the approbation of all.

As they approached the tomb, they found that a brilliant and glowing sheet of snowy whiteness was laid upon it. But as soon as they touched this mysterious, ethereal sheet, it vanished utterly! Lifting the heavy stone which sealed the tomb, they found inside it two caskets. These were of gleaming marble, and one contained the bones of St. Benedict, whilst the other held the bones of his holy sister, St. Scholastica. They were positioned in such a way that their heads were towards the choir area, where all the monks gathered to sing the psalms and sacred chants. Their feet, however, faced the altar consecrated to St. John the Baptist. Moreover, there were three other caskets within the same tomb—one containing the remains of Charlemagne, the Holy Roman Emperor; another

3. A city in southern Italy, on the shores of the Adriatic Sea.

containing the remains of Constantine the Great, the first emperor of Rome who had accepted Christian baptism; and the third containing the body of St. Simplicius, who had been pope at the time of Benedict's birth.[4]

Honesty and regard for strict veracity demand that one unhappy and regrettable incident must be included in the narrative of what transpired that night. For Giorgio, the church warden, not only rejoiced greatly at the sight of these bodies, but was also filled with a compelling desire to take a genuine holy relic of the saint for his own personal possession. So, motivated by a mixture of meritorious piety and selfish avarice, he boldly extracted a tooth from the skull of St. Benedict! This enamel artefact he enclosed in a silver vase, which he kept tucked away in his own bed. But—alas for him—within a few days he was struck by a dire and unexplained illness, which was so severe that he could scarcely even eat or drink.

All his fellow monks were, of course, saddened and concerned at his condition. Having considered the matter carefully, they decided to offer him some frank and fraternal advice. "Br. Giorgio," they said, "you cannot have failed to notice that the commencement of your illness coincided almost exactly with your taking the tooth from the body of our holy father Benedict. Surely, it must be obvious to you that you will not be healed until you return it to him!" And, at last, overcome by conscience and responding to their wise counsel, he placed the silver vase containing the saint's tooth next to his casket in the tomb. And from that moment onwards the illness which had afflicted him so badly began to abate steadily, and after a few days he was restored to perfect health.

One of the monks who had found the tomb of St. Benedict was a certain Benedict de Barrucio. This particular monk was not

4. Simplicius was pope from 468 to 483.

amongst the group of those assigned to keep vigil at the saint's tomb, so he went to bed as usual that night. But as he slept, a strange dream came upon him. In this dream, he saw himself approaching the monastery's church, the Basilica of St. John the Baptist, in order to pray there. But two formidable angels, radiant and splendid, stood guard at the door. As he drew near, one of them asked him, "O mortal, what is your intention in coming here?" He replied that he wished to enter the church to pray. The angels responded in a voice filled with celestial authority, "That is not permitted to you at this time! For now our Queen and Empress, the Blessed Virgin Mary, together with the twelve noble apostles, are all within the church paying their homage to the body of St. Benedict." And the monk looked through the door of the church and perceived that it was filled with a luminous, unearthly splendor, and that voices of divine sweetness could be heard issuing from within.

❁ ❁ ❁

The next day following the discovery of the tomb of St. Benedict and St. Scholastica, the Abbot Desiderius invited all the cardinals then present in Rome to the monastery at Monte Cassino. These gladly accepted his invitation. Then the assembled cardinals, together with Desiderius and the monks of the monastery all entered the church and inspected the tomb. And they all saw clearly and plainly that the bones of St. Benedict and his sister Scholastica were unquestionably present in their tombs.[5] Thus there are multiple trustworthy witnesses to attest both to present and future generations that the ancient abbey of Monte Cassino is indeed and undoubtedly still the true resting place of the mortal remains of these two great saints.[6]

5. A contemporaneous biography of the Abbot Desiderius relates that he had a monument constructed to mark the location of Benedict's tomb, fashioned from fine Cycladic marble and covered with countless priceless jewels. *De Gestis Desiderii*, 937.

6. The author is here evidently wishing to present evidence that the relocation of these bodies, as described in the preceding narration of Adrevald, did not actually occur at all.

ii. Some marvelous events which transpired at the time when Benedict's tomb was discovered

IT NOW BEHOOVES ME to direct my pen[7] to the narration of some marvels worked by the Divine Majesty at the time when the tomb of St. Benedict and St. Scholastica was discovered within the church at the abbey of Monte Cassino.

IN THOSE DAYS, THE future pope, St. Leo IX, was still a small infant. On the night following the discovery of the saints' tomb in Italy, young Leo lay in his cot in the distant region of Alsace in France. Now it happened that a huge toad of a malignant and venomous species had crept into his room. And this monstrous amphibian leapt upon the infant, and bit him on the throat, pouring out its loathsome poison into the wound! Leo's nurse was present, and when she saw this horrendous thing take place, she immediately began to implore the assistance of St. Benedict, with fervent tears and prayers. And the baby Leo, having been attacked by the toad, awoke crying, terrified and confused.

But the nurse then beheld a venerable man robed in a monastic habit surrounded by radiant light. He was descending from the sidereal vault of the heavens, and floating through the air as if he were weightless. This man—who was clearly none other than St. Benedict himself—silently entered through the window. He made the sign of the cross over the boy, who was healed at once from all the ill effects of the toad's venom.

In gratitude for this, St. Leo prayed all seven canonical hours in veneration of St. Benedict each and every day for the rest of his life.[8]

7. This reference to the author of "directing his pen" to narrating miracles ["*ad miracula* (. . .) *exaranda præsens stylus vertatur*"] appears to be somewhat inconsistent with the initial presentation of the history as a talk offered to the monks one evening.

8. This incident is related in a slightly different form in Wibert of Toul's *Vita Sancti Leonis IX*. In that version, Leo was already a boy rather than an infant, and no nurse was present. After being attacked by the venomous toad,

❋ ❋ ❋

[This same Pope Leo IX chose St. Benedict, who had thus once saved his life, as his special patron and protector, and was always animated by unwavering gratitude and devotion to the holy patriarch and a strong supporter of the abbey at Monte Cassino. And Leo continued to experience many miraculous signs of God's grace and favor throughout his life, thanks (no doubt) to the intercession of St. Benedict on his behalf. Of this multitude of wonders, one shall be related here.][9]

It happened that the King of Denmark possessed, amongst his many treasures and curiosities, a particularly splendid parrot. This noble and sagacious bird was blessed not only with glorious, polychromatic plumage, but also the ability to speak with a voice that seemed to be human. Now, when the King heard reports of the great sanctity and wisdom of Pope St. Leo IX, he resolved to send this fine bird to the holy pontiff as a gift. Amazingly, as the bird was being transported it began, quite spontaneously, to say;

> "All ye who hear me, know
> That to the pope I go;
> I'm off to my new home
> In grand and regal Rome!"

And the loquacious parrot continued to repeat these verses without cessation as it travelled along its route to Rome.

After it was presented to Pope Leo, a very close rapport at once sprang up between the pontiff and his new feathered companion. When the bird was first taken into his presence, it is reported to

---

he was sick for several months, until St. Benedict appeared to him and healed him. For the rest of his life, including during his term as pope, Leo was a committed supporter of Benedictine monasteries. Wibert, *Vita S. Leonis,* 470–471. The connection of this miracle to the discovery of the remains of St. Benedict at Monte Cassino seems to be anachronistic, since the discovery occurred (according to this history) during the abbacy of Desiderius (1058–1086), yet Leo IX was born in about 1002.

9. The ensuing anecdote is taken from the *Vita S. Leonis IX.* Wibert, *Vita S. Leonis,* 490–491.

have uttered to him (without any human prompting or training) the following gracious salutation;

> "O Leo, noble pope,
> Our church's holy hope,
> Most blest am I to meet thee,
> Rejoicing, do I greet thee!"

Furthermore, it is reported that Leo, whenever fatigued or careworn with the onerous demands of his pontifical office, would spend time alone with the parrot, and would unfailingly derive great consolation and diversion from his conversations with this singularly talented and precocious bird.

[In his friendship with this parrot, Leo may be seen to have emulated the example of his holy patron, St. Benedict, who did not disdain to cultivate amity, and even to hold converse, with a humble raven.]

❁ ❁ ❁

Now shortly after the discovery of Benedict's tomb at the abbey at Monte Cassino, a group of pilgrims were making their way there, in order to venerate the holy relics of the saint. And as they passed along the road, they met with a certain man attired in the garb of a cleric. They asked him who he might be. To this he replied simply, "I am Peter, the apostle of the Lord." Astonished at this unexpected answer, the pilgrims then asked him where he was going. He said, "I go to visit my beloved brother, St. Benedict, to celebrate my feast day in his company."

Slightly perplexed, the travelers enquired why he did not prefer to celebrate it in his own great basilica in Rome. To this he replied, "Alas, in my own church in Rome there are such gales of turmoil blowing and such strife and confusion afoot, that I cannot celebrate it in peace there!"[10] Now, this day happened to be June 29, the feast day of St. Peter.

10. In the Latin text, it is not entirely clear whether the reference to gales is intended to be taken literally or figuratively. Given the highly chaotic state of ecclesiastical and civil politics in the eleventh century (with up to three rival

Around the time when the holy remains of Benedict and Scholastica were found, there was a certain man named Burello, who was the Count of Castil de Sangro.[11] Now this count was a greedy and impious man, and so decided to set forth on a raiding party against the monastery at Monte Cassino in order to seize by force its treasuries and funds. But as he was passing through the villages of Sant'Elia and San Germano,[12] a tremendous bolt of lightning sprang down at him from Heaven with a fulminant blaze of phosphorescent radiance and a blast of scorching, fiery heat! It struck the spear which he held in his hand, and split it cleanly in two from the top to the bottom.

Following this, Burello was filled with awe and fear of the Lord. Sincerely repenting for his avarice and wicked intentions, he was at once profoundly converted and became a model of piety and devotion for the rest of his life.

Around the same time, the supplies of wine for the monastic community at Monte Cassino began to run low, until their reserve of that rich, rubicund and refreshing fluid was reduced to about the depth of about a handspan and a half within the vessel which contained it. The brother who was responsible for the provision and supply of wine to the brethren went to see Abbot Desiderius, and told him of the impending shortage. Now, at this time, Desiderius was due to make a journey to the court of the local duke, Robert, in the not-too-distant future. And he said to the brother in charge of the wine, "Before I depart to visit Duke Robert, come to see me, and I shall organize for more wine to be purchased."

claimants to the papacy at certain times), it seems likely that a figurative sense is intended. The English rendering offered here has been adapted to clarify this.

11. About forty miles from Monte Cassino.

12. The village of San Germano still exists today. The identity of the other village is not certain, but a conjectural Italianized version of the Latin name has been provided here.

But it came to pass that the monk completely forgot about this. And so Abbot Desiderius departed on his journey, and no order for new wine had been organized. But the same God who provided manna to the Israelites in the desert also provided wine for the monks. For, during the whole time of about three and a half months, this small quantity of wine in the vessel remained apparently undiminished, although it continued to be distributed and drunk by the monks with their usual liberality.

But there was then a certain young boy who lived at the monastery who was particularly inquisitive and perceptive. He noticed that there was very little wine left, but that—by some unknown means—it seemed to continue undiminished, though significant quantities of it were served every day. He was perplexed by this, and resolved to solve the mystery. So he drew a line to mark the level of the wine one day, and came back the next day to observe what had happened to the level of the wine. And it was only once he began to do this that the level of the wine began to decrease. And, pursuant to the normal course of nature, in due course it ran out completely.

When the boy confessed what he had done to the brother in charge of the wine, this wise old monk reprimanded the youngster for his excessive curiosity. "My lad," he said in a tone of kindly reproof, "when we examine too closely the wonders of the Most High and attempt to put his prodigious powers to the test, instead of accepting them with simple faith and gratitude, then they very often soon cease to work for our benefit!"

❁ ❁ ❁

It is told also that in those days the holy patriarch Benedict appeared in a dream to a certain monk of the monastery near the mountain village of Valeria. The saint was accompanied by the ancient martyrs St. Anastasius and St. Pantaleo,[13] who stood at his side. Speaking to the monk, Benedict told him, "Go and see your

13. Both of these saints were martyred during the persecutions of the Christians under the emperor Diocletian.

neighbor, the Count of San Benedetto dei Marsi,[14] and instruct him firmly to return the lands which he has unlawfully taken from your monastery. And you may tell him from me that, unless he does this, he shall die within the space of a year!" For that count had, in fact, taken possession of some of the monastery's fields, motivated by avarice and greed for the deceptive lucre of this passing world.

But when the monk awoke from sleep, he considered carefully what he had been asked to do. Understandably, he felt some hesitancy and trepidation about speaking to the count in such a bold manner, for he was a powerful and notoriously hot-headed man. So, not putting his trust in the vision, he ignored the instructions he had received and did not go to see the nobleman at all.

But a few nights later, St. Benedict once more appeared to the monk in a dream. The holy patriarch reprimanded the brother for his disobedience, and gently slapped his face as a token of paternal discipline. Speaking sternly, he said, "Unless you convey the message which has been entrusted to you to the greedy count, you also shall perish! Surely, that is not something you want." And when the monk arose from his bed the next morning, he found that half of his face—where the saint had slapped him—was covered with the ghastly and disfiguring pallor of the dreaded disease of leprosy!

Filled with panic, he hastened to see the count, as he had been ordered. The count enquired of the monk what was his business and why he had come to see him. And the brother faithfully conveyed to the nobleman the message St. Benedict had given him. "Your Excellency," he declared, "unless you return to our monastery the lands which you have taken from us unlawfully, you shall assuredly meet your doom before these twelve months have passed!"

Having said this, the leprosy on his face at once vanished, and he then took his leave of the count's palace. But various minions of the count, who had heard the monk speaking thus to their master, followed him and hurled sticks and stones at him. The monk turned to them and stared grimly. He warned them thus, "Because

14. About sixty miles from Monte Cassino.

you have treated someone who does the Lord's business with such a lack of respect, your village shall be burnt down!" And that, by the bye, is precisely what happened—for that same year, half of their village was consumed by fire.

The count himself, being a supercilious and stubborn man, was little inclined to heed the admonition of St. Benedict conveyed to him by the monk. On the contrary, he adamantly refused to return any of the monastery's land to them. And although he had been in perfect health until then, he was suddenly struck with a burning fever that very day. Physicians were summoned, but their efforts were of no avail. The fever steadily sapped the count's vitality, and he progressively declined as his mortal life ebbed away.

A few weeks later, as he breathed his last, his final words were, "Alas, since I refused to be separated from these ill-gotten lands whilst I lived, now I am being separated from them, together with all my earthly possessions, by the inescapable and inexorable hand of grim death!" And having spoken thus, he expired. May God have mercy upon his soul . . .

iii. Other wonders occurring after the discovery of the tomb[15]

After the tomb of St. Benedict and St. Scholastica had been discovered at Monte Cassino, it transpired that one of the leading noblemen of Campania,[16] Pandulf by name, was instigated by the promptings of the devil to plan to attack and seize the monastery, and forcibly to take possession of all its estates and property. For this purpose, he assembled a formidable force of knights and soldiers from amongst his neighbors and friends, as well as engaging a considerable body of mercenaries.

In order to keep his nefarious plans secret from the general populace, Pandulf resolved that he, together with his private army, should travel by night under the cloak of stygian darkness, and take their rest (in hiding) during the sunlit hours of day. Indeed, it was his hope that by doing this, no-one should be made aware of his purpose and intentions, and thus the monks at Monte Cassino would not have the opportunity of preparing any defense for themselves. So one evening, after the sun had set, the wicked aristocrat and his forces set forth upon the journey to Monte Cassino.

Thus they proceeded through the whole of the night, until the time of dawn began to approach. At this point, Pandulf sought a concealed place where his small army could set up camp and take their rest throughout the day, before continuing their journey the next night. They came upon an enclosed, isolated field, well concealed by surrounding woods and hills, which seemed ideal for this purpose, and so they set up their camp there.

When evening had fallen, they resumed their journey under the cover of night. Indeed, these wretches, like the sons of darkness which they truly were,[17] had become so blinded by avarice and the

15. This chapter presents only a selection of the more striking cases from the great multitude of miracles contained in the original *Historica Relatio.* Some of these miracles are also related (with slight variants) in the *Dialogues* of Abbot Desiderius (Pope Victor III), which evidently served as a source for the present author. See Victor III, *Dialogi,* 963–1018.

16. A region in southern Italy.

17. See 1 Thess 5:5.

allurements of ill-gotten gain that they ceased to be mindful of the holy words of the Gospel, which declare that, "Those who walk in darkness shall stumble!"[18] They travelled well, and seemed to make good progress. At the end of the night, both men and horses were thoroughly exhausted with the fatigue of their journey.

As dawn approached, Pandulf again began to look for a suitable place where he and his men could rest throughout the day. Again, he found a small, isolated field, well concealed by the surrounding woods and hills. And everyone was struck by how very closely it resembled the place where they had rested the previous day. But looking more closely, they soon realized that it not only *resembled* that place, but that it *was* the very same place! Somehow, although they had travelled hard through the entire night, they had not progressed any distance at all.

Pandulf and his forces were overwhelmed with bewilderment and fear at this inexplicable thing. They concluded, quite rightly, that Divine Providence, by thwarting their efforts to travel, was not granting them permission to fulfil their villainous plans for invading Monte Cassino. Frustrated from their wicked hopes and filled with shame and remorse, all of them—including Pandulf himself—abandoned their ill-conceived venture, and returned quietly to their homes.

[Yet despite the frustration of Pandulf's attempt to raid the monastery on the particular occasion described above, he had been a habitual and compulsive thief throughout his life. The tragic story of the fate of his soul is related below.][19]

There was a small boy by the name of Pythagoras who lived in the vicinity of Monte Cassino. And it chanced that one day (which happened to be a Holy Saturday) he went wandering by himself

18. John 11:10.

19. The following tale relating to the unfortunate fate of Pandulf's soul is taken from the *Dialogues* of Abbot Desiderius (Pope Victor III). Some details have been abridged in the version presented here. See Victor III, *Dialogi,* 978–980.

through the woods. But soon the warm afternoon sunlight waned to chilly twilight, and the gloaming shadows of eventide faded in turn to the oppressive blackness of night, and thus the poor child found himself completely lost and alone in the tenebrous caliginosity of the nocturnal forest.

But suddenly, two men wearing radiant monastic robes appeared before him. They spoke to him thus, "Have no fear, my child, but follow us!" Without any other assistance at hand, Pythagoras was only too glad to comply with this kindly injunction. He followed the spectral monks, and very soon they led him to a small clearing.

In the midst of this clearing there was a pond, filled, not with water, but with a kind of foul, black, liquid mud, bubbling and churning with hellish, fetid ebullience. And out of this mud, there arose a human figure, twisting and turning as if in agony. And each time it ascended to the surface, two hideous swamp-demons would seize it by the throat and prevent it from escaping.

Pythagoras was bewildered and horrified at this gruesome sight. "Who are you?" he asked the human figure, with a tremulous and fearful voice, "and why are you being thus cruelly tormented?" Through the mire of foul mud in which it was immersed, the figure answered mournfully, "I am Pandulf, who was once a great baron in this region. Throughout my life, I was an unmitigated scoundrel, and stole whatever I could, whenever I could. I am here immersed in this filth because I once stole a precious golden chalice from the holy monastery at Monte Cassino. And although, towards the end of my days, I came to repent of my career of wanton theft and brigandry and made every possible effort to restore all I had stolen, that one chalice I neglected to return. Hence I am being tormented now, as you can so plainly see!

"But please, go to my wife and implore her sincerely to return that golden chalice to the abbey on my behalf. For by doing so, she will save my soul from the wretched suffering which I now endure!"

Pythagoras, who was tender hearted, was filled with deep pity at the plight of poor Pandulf. So the next day, he dutifully conveyed the message of the deceased nobleman to his wife, describing his vision in detail. But, alas, his wife gave little or no credence to the young boy's tale. Whether motivated by skepticism or avarice (or a combination of the two), she utterly and flatly refused to return the stolen chalice! And so, for the soul of Pandulf we may only pray . . . .

❋ ❋ ❋

On another occasion, a group of burglars entered the monastery one night. Making their way to the cellar, they eagerly filled their sacks with the choicest produce—salted meat, cheeses and butter. But as they attempted to leave, they found that their sacks had become, quite inexplicably, too weighty for them to carry. Bewildered and confused, and fearing that if they delayed they should be discovered and captured, they abandoned their heavily laden sacks in the cellar and sought to leave the monastery.

The would-be thieves soon made their way to the central courtyard of the monastery. But, in the ebon darkness of the night, they could find no way to get out of the courtyard, for its walls were high and the gates were firmly locked. They stumbled around vainly, until the light of dawn began to glow in the east. At this stage they began to panic, fearing what would happen when the monks discovered them there. But considering their situation carefully, they adopted a policy of feigning innocence. When some of the monks found them in the courtyard and questioned them about what they were doing there, the thieves claimed that they had wandered in the previous day with some workmen, and had been locked in when evening fell. The monks, who were inclined to be excessively trustful of their fellow human beings, accepted this fabricated story and opened the gates to let the burglars out. These then took their leave, taking care to avoid any obvious haste or eagerness to depart, lest they should arouse suspicion. And they went forth on a path leading into the mountains.

All the wicked plans of these thieves had thus been reduced to naught. For indeed, according to that wise proverb of Solomon, "Neither knowledge, nor cunning, nor strategy has any power against the Lord."[20] Nor is human cleverness able to do anything against the God whose wisdom and justice has decreed that all evil should be ultimately thwarted.

A little later, before the gang of burglars had travelled very far away, the cook of the monastery happened to enter the cellar. He was astonished to find there the sacks which the thieves had left behind, overflowing with the monastery's choicest produce. Calling to mind the unknown men who had been discovered that morning trapped in the courtyard, he at once realized that a robbery had been attempted by them. So he sent forth a number of the more fleet-footed and sturdy of the brethren to apprehend the fugitive intruders.

In a little while, the monks overtook the robbers. And—wondrous as it is to relate—when these criminals saw the men of God approaching them, they were all struck with an overwhelming feeling of compunction and repentance. They openly confessed their intended theft, but added that they had not, in fact, actually taken anything from the monastery. However, the monks bound them with ropes and led them back to the monastery for the community to decide how best to handle the matter.

Now, it is indeed a rare thing for a community of brethren to agree unanimously on any matter whatsoever. And some of the monks opined that the would-be thieves should be soundly beaten, both as a fitting punishment for their intended crime and a deterrent to future offenders. But the majority of the monks felt that, as the men had confessed their guilt and the monastery had sustained no actual loss, they should be released without punishment. This wiser counsel prevailed. Not only were the erstwhile burglars set free, but they shared a sumptuous feast with the monks before leaving. And the monks blessed them and wished them well, warning them with fraternal charity to refrain from crime in the future.

20. Prov 21:30.

Discovery of the Bodies of St. Benedict and St. Scholastica

In the diocese of Chieti, at the base of Monte Maiella, there is a community of Benedictine monks known as the Monastery of St. Liberator.[21] In those days, this monastery was subject to the jurisdiction of the Abbey of Monte Cassino.[22] Alas, many of the monks there had become very lax in their observance of the Holy Rule, and the monastic routine of prayer was no longer properly followed.

One night, as the monks were sleeping in the dormitory, one of them woke up suddenly. And a vision of St. Benedict appeared before him, with the holy patriarch enrobed in an ancient monastic habit and displaying a dazzling countenance. Indeed, the phantom of the saint was suffused with an aura of ineffable wisdom and gravity.

He ordered the monk to arise from his bed immediately, which he obediently did. Benedict then said to him, "My son, urgently awaken all your brother monks! Call out to them with all your might, and urge them to leave this building at once. For I know that very soon this entire edifice shall collapse—yes, very soon indeed!" The monk was terrified to hear these words, and did exactly what the saint had instructed him to do. He cried out loudly to awaken the brethren, and told them briefly but urgently about what he had seen and heard. And because no one is incredulous when his own life is in danger, all the monks believed him, and hurried out of the imperiled dormitory.

Once outside, some of the more conscientious monks remembered that it was then time for praying the office of vigils. Alas, thanks to the prevailing negligence and lack of discipline, it had long ceased to be their usual custom to wake up at night to pray this venerable office at all! But now, unwilling to return to the ill-fated dormitory, they went to the chapel and dutifully began the liturgy of vigils. And as they recited the psalms, they heard a

21. St. Liberator was a second-century martyr who was widely venerated in Italy. He is also known by his Greek name as St. Eleutherius.

22. Monte Maiella is situated about 125 miles from Monte Cassino. At the time of writing, the Abbey of Monte Cassino had a very extensive ecclesial jurisdiction, encompassing a vast number of other monasteries throughout Italy.

thunderous clamor coming from outside—for the dormitory did indeed collapse at that time, just as had been predicted.

Afterwards, they all gave earnest thanks to God and to St. Benedict. They also sincerely repented that they had become so lax in observing the monastic timetable of prayer, and resolved to keep it more diligently in the future.

But they noticed that one of their number—a certain very elderly monk—was not with them. So they inspected carefully the ruins of the collapsed building. And there was the missing monk, quite unharmed!

They questioned him about what had happened, and he explained that he had felt too weak and frail to raise himself from his bed. "But," he said, "a man appeared to me, a man whose face shone like the sun and whose beard glowed like pure snow, robed in the black habit of a monk of our order. He held out his arm, and protected me from the falling rubble as it came crashing down about me. He preserved me from all harm, as you can plainly see!" All the brethren who heard this marvelous thing this were deeply astonished, and none of them doubted that the mysterious monk who had saved the old man was St. Benedict himself.

❁ ❁ ❁

One day, one of the monk-sacristans at Monte Cassino lighted an earthenware lamp before the tomb of St. Benedict, and, attaching it to a suspended chain, raised it almost to the ceiling of the church. Alas, the lamp became unfastened and it plummeted heavily to the floor. But, miraculously, the lamp not only remained alight, but was not broken at all, despite its forceful collision with the hard floor. And not only that, but not a single drop of oil was spilt from it . . .

Another time, when Giorgio was still warden of the church (this is the same Giorgio who had once stolen a tooth from Benedict's skull), he noticed a lighted lamp suspended before the image of the Savior, which is in the same church at Monte Cassino. He was slightly perplexed, as it was not usual for a lamp to be burning there. Drawing closer, he saw quite clearly that, though the lamp was suspended high above the ground, it was not affixed to chains, nor rope, nor string, nor physical support of any kind whatsoever, but was simply hovering in the air!

Astonished, he called upon some of his brother monks. They all inspected it carefully, and found that the mysterious lamp was indeed levitating. Each of the monks who saw this attested to the veracity of this marvel, which they very plainly witnessed with their own eyes.

Another time, on the night before the Solemnity of the Passing of St. Benedict,[23] a sacristan of the church at Monte Cassino went to refresh the oil in a lamp that was suspended before an icon of the great saint. Now, it happened that the lamp dropped out of his hand and fell to the floor below. Surprisingly, however, the lamp was not broken, nor was it extinguished, nor was any oil spilt from it. So the sacristan took the lamp, and raised it up again. And yet again, it slipped from his hand, and fell to the ground. And once more, the lamp remained lighted and perfectly intact. And then a third time he raised up the lamp to put it back in its place, and a third time he dropped it! And yet again, it was perfectly intact.

For this to happen once may be considered lucky, for it to happen twice must be regarded as astonishing, but for it to happen *thrice* must be acknowledged as being nothing short of miraculous!

❋ ❋ ❋

In the days before Henry had become Holy Roman Emperor and was still only a duke[24], he once happened to take respite at a certain Benedictine monastery. But he found that the stables there

23. March 21.

24. The Latin text does not mention which Henry is referred to here, but it seems most consistent with the times and events described that it was Henry IV. He reigned as Holy Roman Emperor from 1084 to 1105, and had been Duke of Bavaria from 1052 to1054, approximately coinciding with the abbacy of Desiderius. However, it is also possible (as the learned editors of the *Acta Sanctorum* opine), that it was Henry II (known as St. Henry the Exuberant), who is identified as having been a Benedictine oblate. As he was Duke of Bavaria from 995 to 1002, the incident described here would then have preceded the discovery of St. Benedict's tomb by some decades.

were not large enough to house the extensive retinue of horses he had brought with him. So, in an act of youthful impetuosity and careless impiety, he had some of his steeds accommodated in the brothers' chapel of the monastery, located next to its church.

That night as he slept, St. Benedict appeared to him in a dream. The saint bore an expression that was severe and indignant, and he reprimanded the young duke for daring to place his horses in such a sacrosanct place as the brothers' chapel. Then the holy patriarch took out a rod and deftly struck Henry on the side with it!

When the hapless nobleman awoke, he found that he felt a searing pain in his abdomen where St. Benedict had struck him in his dream. This pain persisted without any relief; and it was not until Henry made a pilgrimage of prayer to Monte Cassino Abbey and implored forgiveness before the saint's tomb there that he was finally cured of it.

❁ ❁ ❁

A certain chieftain of the Normans, Rudolph, resolved to conduct a raid upon the lands of the monastery at Monte Cassino. In this ill-conceived scheme, he was motivated by naught other than an ambition to add to his own wealth and dominions; for indeed, "the love of money is the root of all evil."[25] For the purpose of conducting his villainous raid, he had assembled together a considerable horde of fighters and expounded his plan to them. But on the very day on which he had chosen to launch his raid, he suddenly and inexplicably dropped dead!

It is not to be doubted that this was a clear manifestation of the awesome and inescapable judgement of almighty God. Upon seeing this, all the other Normans were inspired with fear and dread, and felt a new reverence for the monastery. Henceforth none of them dared even to think about invading its lands or seizing its goods.

25. 1 Tim 6:10.

And what is more, over two-hundred and fifty of Rudolph's troops all died suddenly and inexplicably within the space of two years of the death of their avaricious and rapacious master . . .

DURING THE TIME OF Abbot Desiderius, it happened that the monastery at Monte Cassino was very frequently struck by lightning. Desiderius would often ponder this phenomenon deeply and with a certain degree of perplexity, wondering if, perchance, they were unintentionally doing something to provoke the displeasure or wrath of God. Finally, the abbot prayed to God and to our holy father, St. Benedict, humbly requesting that they should reveal to him why it was that lightning struck Monte Cassino so very often.

Shortly after he had made this prayer, as he slept one night, St. Benedict appear to him in a dream. And he assured Desiderius that the lightning strikes were not a manifestation of divine displeasure or wrath; but that, on the contrary, they were nothing other than the snares of the devil and a vitriolic expression of the ancient envy and resentment which the arch-fiend always bore towards the community of holy monks who served the Lord so devoutly and piously there.

THERE WAS A CERTAIN monk of Monte Cassino Abbey called Maio. The following testimony shows how this unfortunate monk was murdered by the trickery of the devil, and how his soul was saved by the intervention of our most holy father, St. Benedict.

Maio had reached a venerable old age, and, on account of the frailties and debilities often associated with that state of life, resided in the infirmary of the monastery. It happened that during the long prayers on the night before Christmas, he was quite overcome with exhaustion and so decided to return to his bed chamber to lie down for a while. As he made his way there, the devil (disguised in human form) appeared to him and said with feigned kindness;

"Agéd father, well I know
Where it is that thou wouldst go.
Let me be to thee a guide;
Follow closely by my side!

"Yea, surely you will not be able to make it to your bedchamber safely through the gloom of this present night unless you have someone trustworthy to escort you. Please, therefore, permit me to lead you." When the old monk heard this, having no reason to suspect the man to be the devil or to be deceiving him in any way, he gratefully acquiesced and let himself be led by the stranger.

Now, as they made their way to Maio's bedchamber in the infirmary, they passed by a large, open window. As they did so, the devil suddenly pushed the elderly brother out of it, sending him plummeting to his death on the pavement below!

A little later, the other monks noticed that Maio was absent. They searched for him for some time, but without success. Then one of the brethren, John by name (the brother of Leo, the Bishop of Ostia),[26] looked down through the open window in the infirmary. To his great disconcertion, he saw the dead body of Maio on the ground below. Calling all the brothers to himself, they were shocked and horrified to see their elder confrere lying defunct. With great sorrow and reverence, they transported his battered and lifeless body back to the main monastery building, to await burial.

Now, there was great confusion and uncertainty in the minds of many of the brothers about how Maio had come to fall out of the window. For it seemed extremely unlikely that it was a simple accident. Had he thrown himself out, in a moment of irrational despair? Or had something more sinister transpired? To solve this mystery, the abbot—at the time the most reverend Oderisius—summoned all the brethren to himself, and called upon their holy father, St. Benedict in humble prayer. He implored that, through

26. A town close to Rome, on the mouth of the Tiber River. This Bishop Leo of Ostia was the co-author of the *Chronicus Casinensi,* extracts of which are presented in the following chapter, and presumably had also been a monk at Monte Cassino.

the intercession of the saint, the same God who had revealed hidden mysteries to the prophet Daniel in the days of yore should now reveal to them how Maio came to fall to his death from the window. And all the monks joined in this prayer, calling upon God with one heart and one soul.

And it happened then that the ghost of Maio then appeared before one of the monks, who was called Placid. This specter spoke to him, and enquired, "Br. Placid, pray tell me, why are you so sorrowful and wherefore so melancholy?" To this the monk replied, "It is not only I who am saddened, but the Lord Abbot and all the community. We are deeply grieved at your death, Br. Maio! And we have been pouring out prayers to Heaven incessantly on your behalf. But please tell me, how did this tragedy come to pass? For surely there must be some explanation as to how and why you fell out of the window."

The phantom of Maio answered him, "Indeed, I was sorely deceived by the devil! For a stranger appeared and offered to lead me through the darkness to my bedchamber. Little did I know that it was a minion of hell disguised in human form. As we passed by the window, the mephistophelian stranger suddenly turned on me and pushed me through. How terrified I was as I plummeted to the ground! And, as you know, the fall was fatal.

"But after I had fallen, the wicked devil seized my soul and continued to lead it along a path that went steadily downward, towards the netherworld of infernal torments. This path was strewn with burning coals, with fiery abysses gaping on either side. And my erstwhile 'guide' not only kept pulling me further downwards, but even sought to shove me off the path into the flaming pits which surrounded us!

"Then suddenly our holy father St. Benedict appeared on the path before us. Instantly, the devil took to craven flight. Blessed Benedict then lifted me up, and carried me with him to a place that was very different indeed—a place of radiant light, sweet music and eternal peace! And there my soul now takes its rest . . . " Once the ghost of Maio had said this, he vanished into thin air.

After Br. Placid had related this marvel to his confreres, they all gave praise to Christ, thanking sincerely both God and the patron and protector of all holy monks, St. Benedict, for preserving the soul of their beloved brother Maio from the clutches of Lucifer and from his hellish realm of eternal suffering and woe.

❁ ❁ ❁

In the city of Salerno[27] there is a monastery consecrated to the name of St. Benedict, which has been under the jurisdiction of Monte Cassino Abbey since its foundation. Now, there was once a ferocious wolf which infested the area, which had regrettably acquired a taste for human flesh. And it happened that a small boy, the son of a local family who was engaged by the monastery as a servant, was captured and seized by this beast.

His mother, seeing her dear son in the snarling jaws of the wolf, cried out to it, invoking confidently the subvention and succor of the saint;

"O wicked beast of sateless greed,
To my warning, take thou heed!
By Benedict, I thee adjure,
Release my offspring from thy jaw!

"Oh, by his bones, I order thee,
Let my darling child go free;
Yea, free him from thy heinous bite,
Lest the saint thy life shall smite!"

Upon hearing this solemn behest made in the name of the holy patriarch, the wolf obeyed immediately and released the boy from his befanged mandible.

But the savage creature then leapt upon *another* boy, and began to attack him instead. In this case—alas!—the unfortunate child was not protected by the patronage of St. Benedict, and so there was to be no happy ending for him. For the wolf promptly bit off the boy's head; and, discarding the remainder of his body, it fled

27. A port city south-east of Naples, about ninety miles from Monte Cassino.

away to its forest lair carrying the detached cranium of its young victim in its jaws.

It once happened that a monk called Arderard, who served as gatekeeper to the Abbey of Monte Cassino, had been away on a journey, and so had to spend the night on the plain at the base of the mountain on which the aforementioned venerable monastery is located. In the middle of the night (according to his own report), he raised his eyes to look upon the abbey, and there he perceived a light shining above it with all the golden refulgence of the noon-tide sun. At first it shone above the church only, in which the holy tomb of St. Benedict and St. Scholastica is located, but then its rays spread more and more, until it illuminated the entire monastery complex. This miraculous luminescence continued to appear for about half an hour, before gradually fading away to darkness.

At this point, Peter the Deacon concludes his discourse to the monks, addressing them thus:

My beloved brethren, it is the discovery of the body of this great and holy man and the revered patriarch of all monks, St. Benedict, which we shall celebrate on the morrow with unbounded joy, joviality and jubilation. As you have just heard, this discovery has been marked by many marvels and wonders, which serve to prove the authenticity of the holy relics beyond any shadow of doubt.

While we are alive, may St. Benedict be our protector and patron. After we have passed from this mortal sphere into the realm of eternity, may he be our guide and guardian, and the defender and advocate of our souls before the most just and clement Judge, our eternal Lord and King, Jesus Christ; to whom be all glory, praise, honor, power and majesty for ever and ever! Amen.

iv. Further visions and signs confirming the authenticity of the mortal remains of Benedict and Scholastica at Monte Cassino[28]

The Holy Roman Emperor, Henry,[29] was subject to a certain cruel and persistent malady which caused him very grievous pains. He was also a very devout Christian, and a frequent visitor to the Abbey at Monte Cassino. And the majesty and splendor of the abbey church there impressed and moved him most deeply. However—as he himself confessed—he did entertain certain doubts as to whether the body of St. Benedict was really present in that church or not.

One night when Henry was staying at the monastery at Monte Cassino, he lay in bed, tossing and turning on account of the pain of his affliction (such was, indeed, an all-too-common experience for him). He was at the time neither fully asleep, nor yet was he truly awake. And, behold, suddenly St. Benedict appeared before his eyes! Henry took this as an opportunity to speak to him. He had long wished to attain certitude as to the location of the saint's mortal remains, and so he asked Benedict to tell him where his body was to be found.

To this, the ghost of the holy patriarch replied, "My son, I know full well that you entertain doubts as to whether or not my body really rests in this venerable monastery. But that all doubt may be dispelled from your mind and that you may know for certain that my bones remain in this very place, tomorrow I shall give you an irrefutable sign! For once dawn has arisen, you shall soon

28. The incidents in this chapter are extracted from the *Chronicus Casinensi Leonis Episcopi Ostiensis et Petri Diaconi Casinensis,* which is included as an appendix to the *Historica Relatio* in the *Acta Sanctorum.* See Leo of Ostia and Peter of Monte Cassino, *Chronicus Casinensi.*

29. As in the earlier reference to an Emperor Henry, the identity of this Henry is not entirely clear. The fact that he is described as being a frequent visitor strongly suggests that it may have been Henry II (known as St. Henry the Exuberant), who was a Benedictine oblate. Henry II died in 1024, which would mean that this incident occurred before the supposed discovery of the tomb of St. Benedict and St. Scholastica. Indeed, this seems consistent with the uncertainty felt by Henry about the location of their bodies.

be freed from that which has been causing you such grievous pains for so long."

Early the next morning when Henry had roused himself from bed, he took his customary visit to the lavatory to attend to the necessities of nature. And as he did so, he passed three small stones or pebbles! These were what are commonly known as "gall-stones," and had been the source of the discomfort which had afflicted Henry for so long. But after he had expelled them from his body, he experienced such pains no more.

Naturally, the emperor offered prayers of profound gratitude to God and to St. Benedict. A little later that morning, when all the monks met together, he addressed them thus; "My dearest brethren, you are all aware of the frightful pain from which I have been suffering for so long! You also know that, thus far, no physician has been able to cure me. Now I ask you this: what should I be prepared to pay to a physician who was able to take these pains away from me?"

To this monks responded unanimously, "Your Majesty, you should surely gladly give whatever is necessary to relieve yourself of this dire affliction! Indeed, we should not begrudge you even the property of our own monastery, if it were necessary or helpful in purchasing relief for you." Henry replied, "Very well! I am pleased to tell you that St. Benedict himself has acted as my physician, and has successfully cured me this very morning. And I shall therefore offer to him the generous remuneration which you have so magnanimously recommended." He then proceeded to narrate his vision of the saint which he had experienced the previous night and what had transpired that morning, even showing them the stones which had been the source of his vexation. Moreover, he declared that any doubts he may once have entertained about the location of the bodies of Benedict and Scholastica were entirely gone, and that he was now absolutely certain that they were, in fact, truly there at Monte Cassino.

Having said this, the noble emperor commended himself to the prayers of the monks. And, in accordance with his pledge to offer generous payment to St. Benedict for his cure, he gifted to the monastery a splendid and beautiful orb of royal purple adorned with Phrygian gold, together with a fine alb and cincture, and a stole and maniple.

His devotion to the monastery at Monte Cassino was such that he very often returned there to visit. Furthermore, he promised that if he lived long enough ever to be relieved of his imperial duties, he would gladly exchange his royal robes for a monastic habit and become a monk of the monastery.

It is also to be noted that, having been made certain by means of his vision and miraculous healing that the mortal remains of Benedict and Scholastica were still safely at Monte Cassino, the emperor commanded that all writings that were found concerning the supposed relocation of their bodies to France be consigned to the flames and destroyed.[30] And he would often publicly relate what the Lord had revealed to him there, demonstrating plainly that the stories of the removal of the saints' relics were entirely frivolous fabrications, fatuous falsehoods and fictitious follies.

Once it happened that the Roman pontiff, Pope Urban II,[31] was visiting the monastery at Monte Cassino. And whilst there, he began to be vexed by certain pains in his side. These pains he very often experienced, and they had troubled him for a long time. It was then the night before the feast day of St. Benedict, and the pontiff lay languishing in his bed, suffering terribly. Now it is to be noted that this pope, like the Emperor Henry, entertained some doubts about whether or not the body of St. Benedict was really at Monte Cassino.

30. This would obviously include all copies of *The Tale of the Relocation of the Bodies of St. Benedict and St. Scholastica into France* by Adrevald of Fleury, included in the present volume.

31. Pope Urban II ruled the Catholic Church from 1088 to 1099. His predecessor had been Victor III, formerly Desiderius, abbot of Monte Cassino—under whose abbacy the tomb of Benedict and Scholastica had supposedly been discovered.

But then St. Benedict himself appeared before him! "Why is it," the saint asked the pope, "that you doubt whether my body is really here?" Urban was perplexed by this sudden apparition and also by the unexpected question. He inquired of the ghostly figure, "Who are you?" To this the saint responded, "I am Brother Benedict! Doubt no more, but believe![32] And so that you may have no cause for uncertainty, when the monks arise tonight to commence the office of vigils, you will be presently freed from the pain which currently afflicts you so sorely." And having said this, he vanished.

And, lo, it came to pass exactly as Benedict had foretold. For as soon as the monks commenced the office of vigils, the pain which Urban had hitherto felt in his side immediately went away, never to return. And when he narrated his vision and cure to the abbot, Oderisius, and to the community of monks, there was great exultation and delight—both at the miraculous cure of their beloved pontiff, and the irrefutable confirmation he had received of the genuine presence of St. Benedict's mortal remains at their abbey.

Now it had, by the time of Urban II, become a well-established practice, especially amongst the French, to celebrate annually a feast of the so-called "Translation of St. Benedict," marking the occasion of the supposed relocation of his body to France. But the reverend pope, after the vision and miracle he had experienced at Monte Cassino (described above), publicly declared the stories of this relocation to be entirely and utterly false. He therefore ordered that the feast of the Translation of St. Benedict should henceforth not be celebrated in Rome.

Accordingly, on the date on which it was customarily observed [that is, July 11], he began to celebrate the liturgy of the ordinary day, rather than that of the feast. But certain French cardinals, bishops and monks who were present with him stubbornly began to recite the liturgy of the feast of the Translation of

32. John 20:27.

St. Benedict instead. Urban was deeply frustrated and annoyed by this, and prayed to God that he would give some sign to them to make the truth of the matter clear. And suddenly a great stupor and confusion fell upon all those who were reciting the liturgy of the feast of the Translation, such that they no longer knew what they were doing or saying!

Greatly astonished and perplexed at this, they then began instead to celebrate the liturgy of the ordinary day. This they found they were able to do without any difficulty or impediment. But then some of the more contumacious of them attempted to return to the liturgy of the feast of the Translation. And again, they found their minds and tongues paralyzed by an inexplicable stupor and confusion. Pope Urban noticed all of this, and gave glory and thanks to God and St. Benedict for making manifest the truth of the matter in such a visible and incontrovertible fashion.

At that time, the abbot and some of the senior monks of the monastery at Fleury happened to be in Rome. Urban summoned them to his presence, and ordered that the altar at their monastery which purported to contain the bones of St. Benedict should be dismantled, so that all might know the real truth of the matter of the location of the saint's relics.

Upon hearing this, they all fell at the feet of the pope in desperate and humble supplication. "Alas!" they cried, "if that altar is dismantled and people learn that we do not really have the remains of St. Benedict at our abbey, we shall be completely ruined! No one shall support us, and our monastery shall be abandoned and destroyed. Please, have compassion upon our wretched plight and spare us from certain annihilation!"

The noble pontiff heard their honest and heart-felt supplication, and was moved to pity. Accordingly, Urban mercifully revoked his demand that the altar at Fleury be dismantled. Nevertheless, he mandated, according to the plenitude of his apostolic authority, that no one should henceforth ever presume to celebrate the feast of the Translation of St. Benedict again . . . .

Editor's Note

The feast of the Translation of St. Benedict continued to be widely observed and celebrated, especially in France and England. Today, the Roman Catholic Church observes two feast days for St. Benedict—one commemorating his death on March 21, and another on July 11, the traditional date of the commemoration of the relocation of his remains to Fleury Abbey. However, the liturgical texts for the feast of St. Benedict on July 11 (which is now classed as the major observance) omit any reference to the tale of this relocation.

Bibliography

Adrevald of Fleury. "Historia Translationis S. Benedicti et S. Scholasticae in Galliam." In *Patrologia Latina* CXXIII, 901–910. Paris: J.P. Migne, 1852.

———. "Vita Sancti Aigulfi Abbatis Lerinensis et Martyris." In *Patrologia Latina* CXXIII, 953–968. Paris: J.P. Migne, 1852.

Clark, Francis. *The Pseudo-Gregorian Dialogues.* Leiden: Brill, 1987.

"De Gestis Desiderii Abbatis Montis Casini, postmodum Victoris III Papae." In *Patrologia Latina* CXLIX, 917–962. Paris: J.P. Migne, 1853.

Gregory the Great. "Vita S. Benedicti, ex Libro Dialogorum." In *Patrologia Latina* LXVI, 125–204. Paris: J.P. Migne, 1847.

Jacobus de Voragine. *The Golden Legende.* Translated by William Caxton. London: William Caxton, 1483.

Jacobus de Voragine. *Legenda aurea sanctorum, quae Lombardica historia nominatur.* Lyon: Jacques Huguetan, 1505.

Leo of Ostia and Peter of Monte Cassino. "Chronicus Casinensi Leonis Episcopi Ostiensis et Petri Diaconi Casinensis." In *Acta Sanctorum, Martii, Tomus Tertius*, edited by Jean Bolland et al., 297–298. Antwerp: Jacobus Meursius, 1668.

Mabillon, Jean and d'Archery, Lucas, eds. *Acta Sanctorum Ordinis S. Benedicti.* Venice: Sebastian Coleti and Joseph Bettinelli, 1733.

Mabillon, Jean. *Annales Ordinis S. Benedicti Occidentalium Monachorum Patriarchae*, Vol. II. Paris: Carolus Robustel, 1704.

Peter of Monte Cassino. "Historica Relatio de Corpore S. Benedicti Casini." In *Acta Sanctorum, Martii, Tomus Tertius*, edited by Jean Bolland et al., 288–297. Antwerp: Jacobus Meursius, 1668.

Usuard. "Martyrologium". In *Patrologia Latina* CXXIV, 9–860. Paris: J.P. Migne, 1852.

Victor III. "Dialogi". In *Patrologia Latina* CXLIX, 963–1018. Paris: J.P. Migne, 1853.

Vogüé, Adalbert de. "Is Gregory the Great the Author of the *Dialogues*?" *American Benedictine Review* 56, no. 3 (2005) 309–314.

Wibert of Toul. "Vita S. Leonis IX." In *Patrologia Latina* CXLIII, 465–504. Paris: J.P. Migne, 1853.

www.ingramcontent.com/pod-product-compliance
Lightning Source LLC
LaVergne TN
LVHW010932100826
845153LV00001B/4
* 9 7 8 1 6 6 6 7 9 6 8 5 8 *